CHAOS

The Art of Resilience

Sarah McDermott

CHAOS
The Art of Resilience

ISBN: 9781919262703 Paperback

Published in the UK by: Inspired By Publishing

Edited by Molly Murray, FlowMagic Ltd

Acknowledgements

To the rule breakers, the dream makers,
the opportunity takers and the non-fakers.
This one is for you.

This book has been written in chaos, through chaos, and — somehow — thanks to chaos. But none of it would have made it to the page without the love, support, and occasional well-timed kick up the arse from some very special people.

First up, to the love of my life, Mr. Sean McDermott. For being my solid gold rock. Thank you for walking beside me through every storm, for reminding me to laugh when it all got too much, and for believing in me even when I doubted myself.

To my beautiful little birds, Laurienne, Genevieve, and Shannon — you are my greatest teachers. You inspire me every day with your kind hearts and your desire to do good in the world. Everything I do, I do with you in mind. Thank you for reminding me daily what resilience, love, and pure magic look like.

Then there's my big birds – Mummy and Lynda. A formidable duo. My inspiration and my cheerleaders, who set me off on a path of empowerment.

And, of course, Daddy Cool – my entrepreneurial nutcase of a father who showed me first-hand what successes *(and shitshows)* look like!

To my late grandmother, the infamous Mary Leaf — thank you for the phrase that has carried me through life: *'You could fall in a barrel of shite and come out covered in gold dust.'* You gave me not just words, but a philosophy.

To Linsey — your loyalty, humour, and straight-talk have grounded me more times than I can count. Thank you for always showing up for me. As well as being my bestie and clubbing comrade through the 1990s and beyond.

To Christine – my dear friend and partner in chaos for many years. You showed me what business for girls looks like, inspired me to believe that I could do anything. And introduced me to a world of sophistication, as you took the Lambrini out of my hand and replaced it with a glass of Chablis.

Angharad – you reminded me that I was born to party and flounce! That one statement changed me from a people pleasing nitwit to a 'do whatever the frick I want to do' rebel.

Special love also to Susie, Emma, Michelle, Pete, Ellie and Sara — your listening ears, joyousness and loyalty have been priceless.

To my long-time indispensable crew — my beautiful tribe of loyal friends – too many to name you all, and I'd hate to miss anybody out, but you know who you are. The ones who've cheered me on, poured me a glass or made me a cuppa when I needed it, and who've never flinched at my wildest schemes—thank you for seeing me, chaos and all. You've kept me laughing, lifted me when I fell, and partied with me like the world was about to end. If giggles were gold, by golly I'd be like Tutankhamun!

To my tribe of mentors and guides, past and present — Jeannette, Lisa, Dani, Patrick, Ryan, Nick, Toni, Rob, Mark — I am blessed to have you all in my life. From those who showed me the spiritual, to those who taught me the strategic, thank you for the wisdom, the bollockings, and the belief.

And to my incredible mentees — thank you for trusting me with your journeys. In guiding you, I've found myself guided too. You've shown me that teaching is really just learning in disguise.

To my team – the wonderful ones who put up with my chaos, clear up the shite and somehow make me look professional!

A huge thank you to our incredible crowd of investors – many of whom have supported us through thick and thin. Always keeping the faith and helping us to keep the knickers on our arses in the most hostile of conditions.

And to my loyal followers – you've walked the path beside me, always cheering, always throwing a kind word of support when I needed it the most.

And now, I couldn't express thanks without a very special mention for Molly Murray, my editor extraordinaire, who has helped me wrestle this beast of a book into something that might actually make sense to the outside world — without losing my Yorkshire twang along the way.

And then of course, not forgetting Chloë Bisson and Sophie Milliken — thank you for championing this book into the world and for walking me through the publishing and audio labyrinth. What a power team to have behind me!

To Alison Bryant Mélone, thank you my friend, you've played many parts — from property pal to proof-reader, you've seen the chaos first hand, and now you've been the final eyes of approval before it goes to print.

With heartfelt thanks to Carol Mcallister and Lucy Montagu-Douglas-Scott, without your generosity this publication might not have even made it to print.

And one last wave to the ninkynonks, witches and trolls — you gave it a go, bless ya, but all you really did was remind me how much I love being kind (and how good I am at bouncing back).

And finally — to you, dear reader. You picked up this book. You came with me into the barrel of shite, trusting there might be some gold dust inside. Without you, these words would just be stories. With you, they become a spark.

Thank you. From the bottom of my heart. I'm truly basking in glorious gratitude right now – every one of you has given my heart a song to sing.

This whole book is proof that chaos can turn to gold — and it's only because of all of you.

Love you all loads,

Sarah Xxx

Contents

CHAOS

When everything collapses, embrace the pain, lean into it, learn from it, ride it like a wild dragon, and it will, in the end, be the making of you.

Introduction

Chaos is rife at the moment.

In all my years, I have never seen such utter mayhem—not just in businesses, but in the whole world around me. From tragic wars to financial instability, we are witnessing record numbers of business closures, marriage break ups, and financial collapses.

People are just falling to pieces all over the shop. Health scares are off the scale. And folks are struggling, really struggling with their mental health.

And sadly, there seems to be a suicide pandemic — as I hear of more and more sudden and heartbreaking deaths at the hands of mental anguish.

And do you know what?

I just wanted to do something about it. To help those who feel helpless.

Being in a place of utter chaos myself at the time of conceiving this book, I realised I had an opportunity in my hand – to teach a method, to forge a path, to hold a torch, to offer a cuddle – a shared heart, a journey's companion, for anybody going through great trauma or upheaval in their lives.

Because the often-unseen thing about chaos like this, is that it comes in as a cloaked teacher.

The illusion of doom, horror and sadness, is often just that – an illusion. What this outwardly monstrous angel really does, is she shines a light on just how utterly unaligned your life is. And if you go in with your eyes wide open, she'll give you every hindsight, insight and foresight that you need to master yourself. To win at life.

And that's exactly what it took, for my big awakening…

What You'll Discover in This Book

No matter where you are right now, this is your opportunity to lose everything you never needed anyway. To let it go.

Throughout this book, I will hold you steady. I will guide you into a calm and beautiful space, from which you can recreate — to design a life that truly fulfils you.

You will learn to face yourself, walk right into the mirror and confront the entirety of your being.

And in that process, you'll discover a radical yet deeply fulfilling way of living—one that harnesses and transmutes the power that can only come from cataclysmic collapse – one which inspires you to reclaim your time, energy, and joy.

Because when chaos strips you naked, you finally get to see what you're really made of.

And that is freaking powerful!

We'll journey together through each phase of CHAOS— Collapse, Honesty, Awakening, Orchestration and Success— and I'll show you how to rise from the ashes with your dignity intact and your head held high, using the 'Rebellion Life Philosophy' – the treasure that I harnessed from my own deadly tornado.

This book is your portal to peace. Not for the faint hearted. It's for the desperate, the damaged, the dreamers, the rule-breakers, and the rebels who refuse to settle. It's for those who feel the pull toward something greater, even if they can't yet put it into words.

It's for the ones who know, deep down, that life is meant to be extraordinary, expansive, and unapologetically authentic.

There'll be work to do in here – hard work. But it'll be the most rewarding work of your life. Inner work.

So, let's start with a difficult but vital question:

If you discovered you had just three months left to live, would you still be doing what you're doing right now? Would you wake up and live today exactly as you did yesterday?

Take a moment. No pressure. Just honesty.

If your answer is no — and I have a feeling it might be — then you're in exactly the same spot as most people.

Except you aren't – you're a whole leap further forwards.

Because you, my darling, are exactly where you're meant to be – on the cusp of transformation. Right here, right now. This book found you for a reason.

As Deepak Chopra said, 'Life is a terminal disease.'[1]

The one thing we can never bank on, is tomorrow. It's the biggest mistake to assume a future that doesn't yet exist. The only meaningful thing we can do is make sure that we are living our truth. Today. In the NOW.

Throughout this journey, your truth will unfold.

I mean, if birth is the beginning of the path, and death is the end, then why the frick do we want to be in the fast lane?

In learning the Rebellion Life Philosophy, you will master:

R - Richness of Life — Discover the true meaning of Net Worth. Lose the attachment to transient materialism and learn to harness the abundance that's available to you right now.

E - Energy and Flow — Live in Flow. Become a Frequency Ninja, where life works with you, not against you.

B - Boundless Awareness — Wake up to your true potential. Recognise and break free from puppet strings and patterns, so you can fully command your results.

E- Emotional Mastery — Become unshakable. Cultivate a state of unwavering serenity so that external chaos never disrupts your internal peace.

L - Limitless Love — Be the one who lights up the room, who turns on smiles, and reflects intense adoration back at the world.

L - Longevity —Shift from merely existing, to thriving in every area of your life, creating a sustainable, joyful, and abundant future.

I - Ikigai — Your deepest reason for being. Discover your true essence to unlock the door to purposeful living and prosperity.

O - Omnipresence — Expand your presence beyond limitations. Learn how to make a meaningful impact wherever you go, without spreading yourself too thin.

N - Nirvana – Experience a life of deep, blissful joy, freedom, and fulfilment. Discover how to stop chasing happiness and instead create your own Heaven, here on Earth, right NOW.

This book is not just about thinking differently—it's about living differently. Each chapter is designed to challenge your old ways of seeing the world, replace imprinted beliefs, and introduce you to powerful new paradigms that will shift your reality.

Each page brings with it a reason to smile again, a new tissue to wipe your tears, and dare I say it – a cause for excitation, even celebration!

You won't just read about transformation—you'll experience it.

So, get ready for a full-blown, Earth-moving shift.

It's time to reclaim you. It's time to dive with me, headfirst right into that pile of shite – and we will emerge, resplendent together and covered in gold dust. I've got you, my love. Even if you're on the other side of this planet. I have your back. My heart is big; my arms are long. My community will hold you up. Be scarred, but don't be scared.

Stop the treadmill, drop the ego, lose the attachments—
it's time to embrace beautiful CHAOS, transmute it, and
above all - have fun!

So come on, take my hand darling, and let's go dance
with the chaos – for this is where the magic begins.

*This is your wake-up call. Are you going to sleep through it or are
you going to flipping well move?!*

Module 1

Collapse

The End is Where we Begin

First there was a great cloud of nothing…

And then it emerged…

What a load of nonk!

Great things never actually start at the beginning. There's always a part right before the beginning, which absolutely *must* happen first.

And that, my dear, is where we are now. The big C for Collapse.

The whispers of creation *always* fall straight from the mouth of the abyss. And the abyss *always* hails from a great cocking-smash-wallop of destruction. The universe didn't just appear on a start line one day, bright eyed and bushy tailed. Absolutely not - there was a heaven-shaking catastrophic explosion beforehand, a HUGE biblical collapse of all that once was.

Collapse is simply the universe taking that decision out of your hands. Enforcing it. Because as humans we are so resistant to change, that we often won't take that leap for ourselves. We cling on in desperation, to the same-old – not realising that the very thing we hold falsely in our highest regard, is that which masks our very greatness.

When your business falls down around you, when your partner of 20 years leaves you high and dry, when you lose your position in a company you dedicated your life to. Or you find yourself at the centre of an unexpected health scare.

It is the universe giving you a massive shove.

These situations, horrific as they may feel, are often the catalyst to magnificence. Every one of them will give you strength and blessings galore – but first you must ride them out. This first module in the CHAOS system will explain exactly how and why.

Learning to surrender and allow that change to flow in, is the most empowering step you can take to self-mastery.

So, take a breath and let me hold you steady, as we leap, tits first, straight into that abyss — let's go meet the incredible power that lies within your chaos.

1

Pivot

Ready or not, here it comes, you can't hide…

July 2024 — I sat pensively in the hospital waiting room, with a knot in my stomach, and an unnerving sadness in my heart.

I had been ill for some time and completely ignored it. You know, when you really should get checked out, when your body is screaming for help, but you back-shelf your health in favour of continuing to spin far too many plates.

Well, I had fallen victim to my own stupidity and was now under investigation for numerous issues. One of them, in particular, being nasty… really nasty. So, there I was, about to receive a potentially life-changing diagnosis, and that's when the penny dropped.

It hit me like a tonne of bricks.

If I had 'the thing', I was probably a goner. By the time you get checked out for this one, you're likely to be beyond help. I was immediately consumed with a deeply gnawing sense of regret. A dark cloud enveloped me, as I considered all my 'could have done's and 'would have done differently's. The sadness was almost unbearable as my eyes fell heavy with desperate tears. I sobbed my heart out, lonely and scared on that cold plastic chair.

I realised that *IF* I was on my final three-month timeline, I would absolutely *NOT* want to spend it dealing with the utter mayhem that I had endured for the past few years. I didn't want to be kept away from my precious family anymore, to forgo time with my gorgeous daughters, Genevieve and Laurienne, and my wonderful husband, Sean. To waste the hours, the minutes, the seconds.

Nor did I want to be constantly chased, squeezed and pulled from pillar to post by all and sundry until I was run ragged. I just didn't want to do it anymore. It could cock off. They could all cock off. This life that I had created? It could 100% cock off.

I realised that I had literally sold my soul to the devil, and I wanted it back.

Regret is something I never thought would affect me. Because I'm a *yes* woman. I say yes to everything. This is a trait that so many of my friends applaud me for — having no bounds and being open to all experiences. I always thought this would leave me with no room for regret on my deathbed. After all, that's what they say, right? That you only regret what you haven't done, not what you have had a go at?

Not true.

You see darling, the thing is, I'd always seen my deathbed as a thing way off in the future. My vision was to build a stunning portfolio of luxury holiday homes and hotels, around Gods own County of Yorkshire, to become a gazillionaire, and employ a world-class team who would take the reins — allowing me to bop around the planet on philanthropic adventures with my family, and do all the rest of the lovely silver-lining stuff of dreams.

But none of that had come to fruition yet. Yes, we had the portfolio, but the freedom was nowhere to be found. Instead, I had created a time-sapping monster. And here I was, absolutely ridden with guilt at the thought of an impending diagnosis. Imagining my daughters' forlorn little faces as I told them that Mummy had sacrificed her one and only opportunity to be there for them throughout their lifehood, trials, and tribulations. I just wanted to wrap them in my arms at that moment and give them a whole world of love.

Ok, so I'm a bit of a hypochondriac, and the extreme fear I was going through was perhaps exacerbated by the excessive Googling of my symptoms.

Still, until that scan and blood test came back, I was facing a terminal diagnosis in my head. And I despised myself for it. I couldn't stomach the fact that IF I did get the dreaded C word coming back at me, then it was entirely my own fault.

I had, over the previous six years, completely disregarded my health in the pursuit of greatness in the business world. The workaholic entrepreneur inside me, driven by my desire to prove my worthiness, had in fact, run me ragged. And I was now a physical wreck.

I had ditched exercise in favour of 16-hour workdays, I was surviving on motorway service station food, and I had swapped days in the gym for dusty building sites.

But even more crushing, I had put family time on the back burner.

But guess what? By sacrificing these things and saving them for the future, I had essentially given them up – traded them for 6 years of stress, anxiety and financial burden. And for what?

I could not remember a family holiday where I hadn't spent a good portion of it on the phone. And this broke my heart into a million pieces. The maternal ache and longing that I felt in that moment was unbearable.

My head span, and the nausea engulfed me, as I realised that I had spent my time, all of it, racing along on a crazy treadmill. Following the path that property entrepreneurs before me had paved. Copying 'the model'. Trying, sometimes fruitlessly, to prove myself as a woman in a male dominated industry. Striving to be the best – to validate my existence.

I had forsaken time with my precious loved ones, so that I could be perceived as a high achiever by circles of people I hadn't even heard of before I jumped onto this bandwagon.

I was a puppet. I realised it right there and then. This wasn't the freedom I had set out for.

Yes, Sean and I might have built a whopping great portfolio of luxury holiday homes and hotels from scratch - we literally went from zero to over £22 million in six years.

And yes, I might be known as the expert in my niche in the property world. But none of this mattered one iota when faced with potential death. All of these things are just ego-based nothingness.

As my grandma used to say; *'you come into this world with nowt, and you leave with nowt.'*

I had been entrapped by my own materialistic and ego-centred desires. I was Pinocchio[2] mid-transformation—as he turns into a donkey, under the weight of all this excess - work, stress, striving, excessive everything! Except no Pleasure Island in sight!

I realised I was on a rollercoaster that I had built. It had gotten out of control. Hurtling downhill at breakneck speed!

I wanted to get off. So desperately!

And that was my pivot. If I really had just three months left, I did not want to spend it doing more of this. Hustling for finance, battling the market, desperately trying to get through developments in extreme conditions.

This is where it had got me – in a hospital waiting room. Faced with my fate. And I didn't want it.

I yearned to spend every moment loving my children and husband — to travel with them to Japan and sit beneath the cherry blossom trees. To the foothills of the Himalayas, to study meditation and live humbly like Julia Roberts in *Eat, Pray, Love*.[3]

I was desperate to scoop up my beautiful babes and whisk them off to mystical lands about the globe, to hold hands and dive into the calming blue Mediterranean, enveloped in pure healing saltwater, breathing in the freshness of life.

And I wanted, in fact, to write. This was my true passion, and I'd suppressed it for years, in favour of building a business.

I'd be mortified if I died without writing a book.

There was so much yet to do! I thought long and hard about it. How, if I had another chance, I would look after my body, drink green smoothies, do yoga, meditate more, walk every day, connect with nature, volunteer and do good things to help others.

All of these beautiful thoughts began to light up the dark that had overtaken my mind. And then I smiled.

In that moment, the words just poured out of me.

I picked up my phone, and I wrote this poem into the notes:

The Rebellion

Get out of the 9-5 job, they said.
Buy a zillion properties like Rob, they said.
Flash your wares like a nob, they said
And Network with the right mob, they said

10X yourself like Cardone,[4] they said
Build an Empire from your iPhone, they said
Get pumped and stay in the zone, they said.
Don't stop until you have grown, they said.

Hustle to get on a stage, they said
Pitch and treble your wage, they said
Dominate and become a Sage, they said
Provoke and please do outrage, they said.

They said all of this, to watch the fools
Who do not dare rewrite the rules
They're lured with visions of fancy jewels,
Of fairy castles and private schools.

They said all of this to watch them fight,
To compete for the almighty right
To say that they're the absolute best at 'blah'
To show their 'net worth' with a fancy car.

But what is the true price they pay for this?
A pressure pot life? That sure ain't bliss!
A trophy wife who you're paying to kiss?
A former life with the real friends you miss?

Think about how you leapt out of the job
To run on a treadmill controlled by the mob
Who groom you until you become the nob....
And then you sob.

Or you could say Noooooooooooo!!!!!!

Write your own rules,
Suffer no fools,
Draw your own path,
Do your own math!!!
Keep your true friends,
Make some new friends,
Own your passion,
BE the fashion,
Live in the flow,
Let your soul glow.
And your joy will grow
As you Star in your own show!!!
For you can become a thrillionaire,
Whilst living a life extraordinaire,
That's of your own choosing,
Dreams are for perusing,
So, honour your time
And make life divine!!!

*Written by Sarah McDermott, burnt out entrepreneur,
in Pinderfields Hospital, on a cold plastic chair, whilst
wearing a very soggy-sleeved jumper.*

It struck me that the 'They' in my poem was, in fact, me. I was the one who had heard the words, seen the model, learned the way – and pasted it into my mind, over the top of my actual dreams – like cheap wallpaper.

And then came the rage, the rebellion, the fire. I realised that I could see my true life's pattern emerging through the torn blown vinyl of somebody else's life. And that, my friends, was my awakening.

I took a smooth wooden cross out of my handbag, I closed my tear-stung eyes, tilted my face up to 'traditional God,' and I said a little prayer — in fact it was rather a long prayer, more like an explanation to 'The Universe' and my 'Higher Self,' detailing exactly how I would behave and what I would do differently if I could just have another chance at life.

I pleaded and vowed and expressed my extreme gratitude. I promised to do only what really served from now on.

To live for the now.

And then I waited …

And waited…

And waited some more. That was a long wait. I could hardly breathe the entire time.

But to my absolute relief, my prayers were answered.

The results came back. I didn't have a life-threatening illness. I couldn't believe how lucky I was. I would live to see another day. I sobbed some more!

I did, however, receive a diagnosis of a fatty liver, with cysts and stress-induced gastritis. So, I was in no way being let off scot-free for the abuse, gluttony and stress addiction. But it could have been so much worse. This was the wake-up call that I needed!

As I sat there in my moments of shock and relief, I analysed and unpicked myself. And I came to the realisation that I could find a way to redesign life as something that brings joy, love and prosperity – without the suffering.

It wouldn't have to be difficult, painful or tiresome, and it definitely wouldn't alienate family and friends.

I realised that I could and would say NO to all of the fakery I had enrolled in.

I could rebel, go against the grain, push back on the utter nonk we are sold in the business world. I could flip the switch.

I could forge a new path, shake things up, turn my back on those outdated ideas that are, quite frankly, not serving anybody. And if I did that, then life could be fun, business collaborative, and relationships exciting. And time, health and wealth, would come more easily, more freely and even more abundantly. I pondered on this for quite some time, and one by one, the insights came to me. I knew what I must do to change the trajectory of my life. It would start right here.

So here I am, taking control and ticking off one of the biggest regrets that I would have if I died tomorrow. I am writing this book. I am writing it for me, and I am writing it for you, so that you don't fall foul of the same self-annihilating patterns that I have followed.

At Pinderfields, my wish was granted. I wasn't terminally ill, and in that moment, I vowed to keep my promise...

From then on, I was going to live for JOY! Pure JOY!

In one of my darkest moments, a close friend said to me 'Sarah, you were born to party and flounce.'

And I thought, *damn right, lady!*

It was time to remove the stress and wear a dress!

Time to wake up every morning and smile. Feel the love. And plan my life around family, friends, fun and all the other good stuff that doesn't send you to hospital!

I had seen myself from above.

I witnessed this sad lump of regret sitting there in mental anguish, and I realised that I had gotten here by following somebody else's path.

In seeing that, I was also smacked in the face by reality – and that reality was that it was, and always had been, my own choice. It might have been a wrong choice. But it was my choice.

And then of course came the revelation that I could also choose to get off the freaking treadmill, stop the rollercoaster, leave the rest of the sheep in the field, and just say no.

So, what do we do darlings when we realise that we have been instruments, playing to somebody else's tune? Well, we rebel.

2

Chaos

When life yells: 'Surprise!' – but forgets the cake

Before we continue, I'm going to let you in on a little secret: It's September 2024 and I am talking to you right now directly from the eye of the storm.

This is not a retrospective tale of *something that once happened*. The teachings within this book come straight from the horse's mouth — this mare is currently being flung, knickers in the air, through the stratosphere in an 'Oz-worthy' tornado. Yes, I'll surely edit this chapter, months from now, and add in some hindsights. But this little section, right here – comes from a place of head-spinning turmoil.

I am the experiment, the teacher, and the student.

My biggest lesson so far? That your most powerful asset is the ability to control your emotions and your reaction to the chaos all around you.

Because every new beginning starts with chaos, there's simply no getting away from it. The only choice is to lean in and go with it. No matter how utterly terrifying that thought is.

Even when the floor drops out from under you. When the walls fall over, too – and even the roof blows off. When you are completely side swiped by the unexpected.

It's the force that shatters certainty into a squillion-piece puzzle, and demands complete and utter, painstaking, reinvention.

Why are you here with me now? Reading or listening to this book? What force walked you into the bookstore? Or drew you to this title on Audible?

Why have you chosen to hear my words? To walk with me along this unfathomable path?

It goes without saying that the title, *CHAOS*, resonated with you in some way. I'm guessing that you've suffered a great loss? Or that you're in the midst of madness, mayhem or melancholy. Whether your marriage has ended, your business has collapsed, or you're having an almighty existential crisis, there's no doubt in my mind that you've been knocked off your feet by some cataclysmic shift or other in your life.

And chaos is always the instigator. She's a naughty one!

I've always had a strange love affair with chaos. People say she follows me. And they might be right.

For years and years, I have had a close association with this beguiling word. I even wear it on my heart, literally - one of my favourite Vivienne Westwood dresses has '*chaos*' emblazoned on the front of it.

People say that I am chaotic, and that chaos ensues when I am around – perhaps in reference to the wild, exuberant and hedonistic parties that I have thrown over the years! Haha! But nevertheless, chaos excites me.

Even typing the word now makes my heart flutter. My whole physiology is lifted by this word that terrifies most.

Why?

Partly because I'm a rebel, who doesn't align with conformity, rigidity, order and rules. But more than that, chaos is, to me, the starting point of all great things. It's an opportunity to blast the past into smithereens and start again. To erase the whole narrative. To press delete on all that you have known. And to begin again.

It's like when you decide to completely reorganise your wardrobe. What happens first? Absolute fricking chaos ensues, that's what! As everything is dumped, chucked and launched all over the floor. (At least this is my method!)

Only when you have all of your worldly goods laid out in front of you, can you see the obvious order that needs to happen. Suddenly new systems pop into your head. You have created a void. A space. A huge, empty shelf of potentiality. And now you have the opportunity to reorganise, declutter, and throw out the things that no longer serve you.

And when you have finished? You have a super slick, new representation of your life. Your bestie comes round for dinner, and you CANNOT wait to show her your tidy new dressing room, all colour-coordinated and neatly folded. Not a single bra-pad in the sock drawer!

This is a great feeling. You are proud, empowered, and life seems to flow much better when you know exactly how many black thongs you own.

But without being prepared to dip your toe into some momentary chaos, by daring to pull your threadbare gussets out into the light of day, you'd never open the door to this newfound place of contentedness.

You'd still be stuck with the same old uninspiringly overstuffed wardrobe. If only you'd launch yourself into the cataclysmic void now and then, just for a little while?

What is in your life now, that needs pulling out onto the floor and sorting out?

In every burst of chaos lies the raw blueprint for transformation, urging us to reinvent ourselves anew.

Now of course, the kind of chaos that really changes lives, is a lot more intense than a wardrobe refurb.

I'm here to talk to you about proper chaos. The type of head-spinning, gut-wrenching, heart-breaking stuff that leaves you feeling like you might lose everything – even your marbles. When all that you have known is in doubt. When your world has been smashed into a million-piece jigsaw, and you don't know how the chuff to reassemble this mighty mess.

THAT KIND OF CHAOS.

COVID -19, and its aftershock, created chaos for many in business, myself and my husband, Sean, included.

We clung on to the seat of our pants, desperately awaiting the return of normality. But strangely, that never quite arrived. Instead, we were greeted by something we could never have foreseen.

An internal fraud. An obscene amount of money lost at the hands of a trusted employee with a gambling addiction.

We were completely sideswiped by this devastating blow — aside from feeling utterly saddened and hurt by the betrayal, it stripped us bare, at a time when financially, we just couldn't take anymore.

This, in turn, saw the collapse of multiple finance deals, leaving us literally penniless with two unfinished developments to complete, an expensive business to run, and a closed hotel to cash flow.

This was complete financial crisis territory– aka the type of chaos that sinks ships.

And a sinking ship, along with all of its passengers, who are depending on you to bring them to shore, is one hell of a responsibility.

Despite being armed with a pair of 'big shiny balls' from having come through Covid and 'that budget', for the first time, I felt like giving up. What was the freaking point? I had given my life to this beast, only to be slapped in the face, again, harder than ever before.

Suddenly we were faced with a huge onslaught of unpaid bills. Angry suppliers. Unpleasant conversations and difficult negotiations.

One of our Serviced Accommodation businesses went into liquidation. It wasn't at all pretty.

We went from SA Mastery to SA *almost* Disastery!

And for a short time there, the sun went down on me, and I was plunged into a dark underworld.

I hit rock bottom.

BUT that's exactly where the golden lessons come from.

Nobody learnt to steer a majestic yacht through an epic storm without actually doing it and living to tell the tale.

I was under an immense amount of pressure to not sink
– for the sake of everybody else. And although having
that kind of pressure isn't pleasant – being unable to pay
the trades on the development sites and negotiating with
receivers — it was being responsible and accountable for all
of those other people – my family, our investors, and our
teams – that saved me.

The sheer responsibility held me up and inspired me to
act, at a time when I wanted to crumble.

So, I put my big girl pants on (no, not the black thongs
— these were the kind of support pants that come up to
your tits and down to your knees), and I took the helm.

What we went through then, and are going through
now, is the greatest personal growth period of our lives.

This is/was hardly a passing shower, it's been a Biblical
monsoon – relentlessly blasting us, month after month, as
we forge our way ahead, hoping to reach safety. Hauling
this great hunk of responsibility to the shore.

For now, our business is afloat. And although we are
still out in the water, we do have a set rescue plan, and
so long as we stay focused, level-headed, and open to
opportunity, there's a great chance of success.

But going back to that lesson: *Your most powerful asset is the
ability to control your emotions and your reaction to the chaos in
the world all around you.*

When you learn this art – you will hit a whole new level of success.

Success that transcends any business.

The greatest success of all – the conquerment (yes, I've just made that word up) of oneself.

This is where you locate your internal control panel, you find the ability to stay strong under pressure, to command every outcome. To experience deep peace, joy and fulfilment in ANY circumstance.

You can't buy an awakening like this on a course.

You can read about it in this book, yes, but you can only achieve it by being ripped to shreds to expose the light within.

Chaos shouldn't be feared. It turns coal into diamonds.

Fear and anxiety mask the multitude of gifts that chaos is here to deliver. So, for goodness sake, lose the bloody fear. Lean into it, with your eyes wide open. Seek the centre, the cause. Sit in that place and observe until it starts to make sense.

According to ancient Greek mythology, chaos *(khaos)* is, in fact, the primordial state from which the universe itself was born.[5] And although chaos denotes a state of disorder, digging deeper, we see that it also encompasses potential, transformation, and the seeds of order.

Chaos is a heck of a lot more than disorder. It is the catalyst for Transformation and Renewal.

It invites you to dig deep, to question your reason for existence and to realise your true potential.

It's a chance to reincarnate without physical death. Just the death of a previous, potentially toxic or stagnant, way.

Chaos takes us into the unknown, to face our fears head on. It often brings with it terrifying moments of loss of control or perceived failure. But in fact, that exposure to intense fear, results in resilience and strength.

It is the key to expansion.

It's in those moments of utter 'shit has hit the fan' when you realise that no matter how bad it is, the world keeps turning, there's still a roof over your head, food in your belly, and somebody loves you.

So actually, it's never all that bad. This is when fear starts to lose its grip on you, especially the fear of loss of material items. And then you step into your power.

That is when you welcome chaos in.

You are here with me now, in the midst of our real-life chaos. You are the witness to the emerging awakening, to a new philosophy for life, birthed directly from the darkness. And you, my dear, are with me on the journey through:

C – Collapse

H – Honesty

A – Awakening

O – Orchestration

S – Success

This is not a mantra of inspiration, it's a safe, and guided path. It's a model that will lead you through these pages and guide you back to yourself.

Each module is a revelation that will see you breathing relief, pushing your boundaries, opening your eyes, and striding confidently into your life-long joyful, and truly purposeful place.

Right now, we are in C 'Collapse'. But there is no short cutting the HAOS. So, you need to be brave, put your big girl pants on, and hold my hand if you need to, as we prepare to go deep.

Understanding chaos is absolutely necessary for your development, in business and in life. Lean into it. Work with it. Learn from it.

When chaos crashes through your door, thank her, don't resist her. Invite her in, have a chat, and ask what she's here to teach you. Because the best success stories really are born from the ashes of the old.

In one of my favourite childhood films, *The Neverending Story*,[6] the great Nothing sweeps in and destroys everything. At first, there is an eerie silence and complete darkness. But then there's a flicker of light.

It highlights a few fragments of what once was – floating around in the void.

Then, the Oracle appears. She speaks with trembling sadness in her voice, until she delivers that great revelation that the only 'thing' that matters, that could never be taken away, and the ONE thing that has the power to create everything from scratch, is the reader.

And that reader is you.

You are, in all of this, the only thing that really matters. You can lose material wealth, you can lose your business, your relationship can come to an abrupt end, but you can never lose the wisdom etched into your soul. You are the story.

And you're still writing it!

So, what are you going to create next?

How are you going to make your next creation bigger, better, and bombproof?

How are you going to find peace within the loss, and build a life of joy?

What would you actually do with your last three months?

And how are you going to make every three months, every day in fact, just as purposeful as if it were your last?

It's time to find out.

3

Get SET

Making the best of a bad situation by Sarah McDermott!

I'm going to start by saying this loud and clear for all to hear:

I LOVE CHAOS!

There you have it! I don't want to erase a single one of the challenges. They were all meant for me. I own them. The road might have been a bumpy one, but it's *my* road.

If I had a pound for every time I've consoled myself by thinking, 'oh well, it'll make great material for the book' then I could probably retire!

After all, hard times create strong people. And good times, well they create a fricking BORING story, don't they?

But with chaos comes the inevitable first stage, the C in CHAOS and the madness behind this module - Collapse.

And the collapse, no matter how heart-breaking, is entirely yours too. You must accept it – even when life pulls your pants down and publicly bares your arse.

I've realised that surviving chaos is about facing life head on. With raw authenticity. It's about taking it all, accepting the blame. And then pulling out every stop to fix it.

It takes everything to collapse around you, all of the walls to fall in, for the real world to be exposed in its full, vibrant glory. It also reveals YOU. When there is nothing else to fall back on. You become all that is. And that is so powerful.

Once you go through something like this, you really do begin so see life from a higher place. You can literally look down on yourself and see how much of a game it all is.

So why do we invest so much time whinging and moaning about every minor 'botherment' that interrupts an otherwise tedious life?

"Most people consider life a battle, but it is not a battle, it is a game."[7]
— Florence Scovel Shinn, *The Game of Life and How to Play It*

We are programmed to love playing the game. Overcoming obstacles, creating solutions, and getting ourselves out of tricky situations. So, let's not act all surprised when the universe delivers more of what we have always thrived on.

We often convince ourselves that next year, everything will be better.

You can only tell yourself this so many times, before naivety turns into wisdom and you realise that the elusive 'easy life' ain't coming.

The truth is that when you overcome the shit show, you are swiftly rewarded with an even bigger ordeal.

This is the game of life.

I like to think of it as a computer game. You beat the baddies in level 1, so up you go to level 2. Does it get easier? Do you get to sip margaritas in the Maldives, served by a hot waiter-bot? *Do you buggery!*

You get bigger baddies, so you have to get your bigger guns out, my love.

You can't stop the trials, but you *can* enjoy the ride.

As for life's confrontations? These gifts in wolves' clothing are how you will find your peace.

So, join hands with adversity, stay calm and be prepared to lose everything. Including your ego.

Because it's in the action of letting go that we realise our strength.

Become a humble servant, prepare for the chaos – and trust.

The Universe always had my back. That day, I pulled the cross out of my bag and prayed for another chance. I was blessed with exactly the right chaos—whether I knew it or not. It was always my perfect storm.

For us, it didn't happen with the slow-motion inevitability you might imagine. It happened with a sickening speed, like being pushed off a cliff while tying your shoelace.

When the fraud was first uncovered, we were already standing on cracked ground. The cashflow was tight, the developments were mid-flight, we had come, quite miraculously through the toughest period in hospitality development. And I had dared to believe that 2024 was going to be the year we turned the corner.

That illusion shattered overnight.

The aftershock of that betrayal was not just a financial fallout—it was full out war. A relentless series of battles with finance companies and institutions who responded to our temporary crisis not with support, but with threats.

Proposals were rejected. Arrears snowballed. Mortgage payments missed because we chose to pay staff and keep people in jobs.

It meant dealing with credit control departments who gave no hoots that we had essentially been victims of a crime, not understanding that we were already living inside the worst-case scenario.

Many of our investors stood with us—but one took to Facebook with a defamatory attack, and another issued a bankruptcy petition against Sean and I. Statutory demands arrived like venomous letters. Receivers were threatened, in one case, even instructed.

All the while, people stepped forward to 'help'—some well-meaning, others self-serving—each offering their opinion, their prediction: 'You're too far gone. It's over.' And I had to stand there and say no. Over and over again. Even when my voice trembled. Even when I wasn't 100% sure they were wrong.

I had to hold up the damn walls myself—arms outstretched; feet planted in the middle of a collapsing house—just to stop the roof from falling in. And that level of resistance? That level of responsibility? It takes its toll. It creeps into your cells. It keeps you awake at night, gripping your heart like a steel clamp. Feeling it could stop at any moment.

But it also wakes something up. Because in the quiet moments—when everyone else has left the room—you realise it's your house. No one else is coming to save it.

I have never felt so alone, with everything collapsing all around me. I felt completely helpless.

Sean and I lost our income overnight. We had to move out of our beloved family home.

One of the businesses went under.

Our 'excellent' credit scores went down the pan, and with them our ability to raise fast finance. Our reputation was harmed.

The gossips had a field day. I was even dropped from a speaking gig—apparently, I couldn't talk about wealth while weathering a storm.

And to top it off, my health took a hard hit.

So, I pulled out of life, cancelled everything that wasn't crisis-level essential, and went head-first into the abyss.

It was the trial of all trials.

And yet… from this cold and empty space, something unexpected and magical emerged.

Clarity.

I had to analyse the ongoing business not from a place of panic or people-pleasing, but from calm, clinical knowledge.

I stopped reacting to what others thought might happen and instead rooted myself in what I knew to be true. I looked at our model with honest eyes—I saw its weaknesses, but I also saw strength. Even in collapse, it held. Even under pressure, it was performing.

While finance companies made their threats, I made a new plan.

While others saw disaster, I spotted opportunity.

The pressure has squeezed new revenue streams out of the cracks. The management company is reborn under a new brand. The operational systems are leaner. The sales team, stronger. And I'm not saying the new business model is bombproof—but it's better.

We've faced every failure mode a hospitality business could endure, and we're still standing.

But let me be clear: it has taken everything.

There were moments I thought I wouldn't make it. When I broke down, weeping on the floor. There were times when my health gave way, and I ended up in hospital. The thought of losing everything—my family's future, my daughter's sanctuary, the dream we've sacrificed for—was unbearable.

But I haven't buckled. Not this time.

And that's not because I'm stronger than most. It's because, in the quagmire, I came up with a technique to come through the collapse. This technique was the starting point that grew into the CHAOS framework of this book. And I'm going to share it with you right now.

When challenges arrive, it's time to go into crisis mode – and Get SET.

S - Survive – This is the only thought that should be in your head right now. Survive. Just breathe. And put one foot in front of the other.

If you are really struggling, and your thoughts are very dark, please go straight to the resources in the back of this book for links to professionals who can help you. You will get through this.

The main aim of 'Survive' is to steady yourself. This is when you are in panic mode, and you need to calm down. Dunk your head in cold water (seriously, it works) go out for a long walk – without your phone.

Take yourself out of the situation and into a space where your nerves can recover, your physiology can rebalance, and you can start to feel like yourself again. It's so important – by learning to hold your nerve and stay calm, you'll be able to make the most intelligent decisions, backed by decisive action, to help you survive.

I was listening to an audiobook recently, called *Bulletproof*,[8] by Evy Poumpouras, an amazing female special agent who was in the World Trade Centre at the time when the planes hit.

She says in that book that it's often not the disaster that kills; it's panic. She recites the tale of a fellow agent who drowned in a helicopter crash, just because he was overcome with panic and was unable to release his seatbelt – a simple action that he had performed countless times.

You see, when we go into panic mode we can't think straight. We don't see the obvious solutions. Fear engulfs us, controlling every action we take. The first stage of successfully riding out a chaotic event, is to survive. Survival means staying calm.

You'll perfect this in the upcoming modules.

E - Evolve – Once you have come through the 'life or death' phase, you can now harvest the hindsight from this unpleasant period. It's time for deep reflection.

Ask yourself the following questions:

- Why did this happen?

- What did I NEED to learn from this?

- How did I contribute to it happening? What can I do next time to avoid this?

Get your journal out here and really analyse in fine detail everything that has come from this, the good, the bad and the ugly.

You might be really surprised at how much good there is, in the end. As we move through this book, you'll uncover methods to go deeper and identify those golden nuggets.

Use these techniques to plan your rebuild. Bigger, better and stronger.

T - Thrive – You have now learnt something really valuable. You are stronger, wiser and more resilient. From here you can make a new plan and take decisive action.

It really is survival of the fittest, and you will thrive for coming through this challenge.

The prize is the wonderful glow of empowerment. It is under immense pressure that coals become diamonds, and you my darling, are becoming a precious stone!

Next time disaster strikes, just think back to the Get SET steps: Survive, Evolve, Thrive. You will be SET for success every time!

Now then, hold that thought, you may feel empowered for that fleeting moment when you 'survive'. But with most storms, comes trauma. And sometimes, the trauma wound cuts deep.

Body builders use repeated muscle trauma to create beautifully sculpted silhouettes – just as you can use mental trauma, to develop your own masterpiece – YOU.

Let's delve into that, right now.

We're in it together. I've got your back.

4

Trauma

The Aftershock

You don't walk away from chaos untouched.

You might survive the collapse, rebuild your systems, and make new plans—but the trauma? It lingers.

It shows up at night.

After the champagne has been chinked, after the adrenaline wears off. That's when it creeps in. The empty feeling in your heart. The violation. The strange fears that weren't there before, holding you back to 'protect' you from similar dangers.

So, before we move out of Collapse, we need to talk about what gets left behind when the storm passes.

Trauma.

The most potent thing you can do with trauma is transmute it.

Ask most highly successful people about the catalyst for their success. More often than not, it is some kind of trauma.

Whether they've lived through war, poverty, loss or betrayal, there is one thing that is very clear—trauma gives birth to resilience.

For those who have survived trauma like this, the world can feel unsafe, unfair, and overwhelming. And yet, when you look at many of the most successful people on this planet, you'll notice a pattern: trauma isn't just something they endured.

It was the catalyst for their transformation.

Trauma continues to haunt through memories and triggering experiences. But those who have survived great adversity often go on to master life.

Because once you have lived such hardships, you can handle most things. Life is all about perspective.

A child who has never known trauma might be distraught when his ice-cream falls on the floor, whereas the child who has lived through poverty and abuse might be grateful for the couple of licks he had before it fell, or even just warmed by the person who bought it for him.

If you are a trauma survivor, it is likely that the 'damage' will be written deeply into your story. It undoubtedly shaped the curve of your path—violation might be told on your face or betrayal, hidden in the depths of your heart. It will be with you, always, and to try and suppress it and deny it, is rarely the right way to lighten your life.

Trauma can be worked with. No matter how hard-hitting and appalling it was at the time. You are here now, and this is an opportunity for you to alchemise the hurt, the pain, the anger into power. Pure personal power.

If you've had to endure the unthinkable, and you have lived through it. You have the right to release the sadness and the hurt.

The truth is that resilience is trauma alchemised.

Fact.

All resilience comes from trauma. Nobody builds mental or emotional strength from a life of ease. It's forged in fire. In pain. In heartbreak.

That means that every painful experience you've ever had is actually a deposit into your strength savings account. It's a painful blessing, but a powerful one—if you let it be.

You can use trauma literally as a superpower. All emotion carries energy. The more intense the emotion, the more forceful the power behind it. And that is why trauma, once harnessed, can turn you into a superhuman.

It doesn't mean you go looking for more pain, but it means you harness what you've already endured and turn it into gold. When you alchemise your trauma, you become the one who *can't be shaken*, who sees through the chaos.

True resilience is not about pretending everything is fine. It's about knowing you've lived through the worst, and you're still here. It's the deep cellular knowing that no matter what happens—you will handle it. You've handled everything so far. You are unshakeable.

The key to releasing any internal lingering trauma, no matter how big or small, is forgiveness.

Forgiveness isn't about saying what happened was okay. It's about choosing not to let it define you. It's not about them—it's about freeing yourself from the weight of the past.

Anger, resentment and blame are completely toxic feelings that will eat away at your insides. Feeling hatred towards another person really is like drinking poison and expecting the other person to die.

So even if the person who did something to you is an absolutely vile human being, for your own sake, you need to release the attachment.

As a young woman I was sexually attacked. I had counselling at the time; the lady was nice enough, but it didn't heal the trauma. I was put on antidepressants which were hideous, I took one, felt terrible and decided to carve my own path to emotional freedom. I appreciate that antidepressants might work for some, but for me - they had the opposite effect.

I was only 19 when my friend bought me a meditation tape. It was my first introduction to mindset work. But when I went into that space, I found peace, for the first time since the attack. I managed to carry on with my life.

But I did then attract a stream of violent boyfriends – I was clearly still blaming myself for the incident and believed that in some way I deserved it.

I needed to forgive myself. And I needed to forgive the attackers too. It was years later when I realised this and decided to forgive the perpetrators, wholeheartedly.

I released myself from victimhood, I just decided I did not want to be a victim. I wanted to be in control of my own life, and that couldn't come whilst I was hanging on to my victim story.

I needed to accept that what happened was just a part of my journey. I had survived. I had an awful lot in my life to be grateful for. And I wanted to crack on and enjoy it.

You can carry trauma for the length of the event—or for a lifetime. But who wants that? You don't deserve it.

You didn't choose what happened. But you can choose what happens next.

So, forgive. And most importantly forgive yourself. For your perception that it might have been your own fault, for carrying the weight of it thus far.

Forgive yourself completely. Start showing yourself love. The late great Louise Hay often shared her mirror technique – locking eye contact with yourself in the mirror and telling yourself 'I love you'[9] and 'I approve of you'.[10]

I used this technique myself and still do. It's a great resource. You might feel silly at first, but it actually works, so please put your inhibitions aside and give yourself a chance!

If you're struggling with forgiveness, the next step is to seek a trauma coach who resonates with you. Perhaps somebody who has been through a similar experience themselves. They will be able to hold your hand and help you to come through the darkness into a space where you feel you are able to not only move on, but to reclaim your empowerment.

Once you do that you will be more self-assured and capable than you ever have been in your whole life.

Sometimes people make choices that others can't understand. But be empowered enough to push the hurt aside, and practice forgiveness.

Because that's the fastest route, for your own sake, to peace and true happiness.

The soul knows her own freedom. Now it's time for you to claim it. Because collapse doesn't end when the fires burn out. It ends when you alchemise what was lost into something greater. When you choose forgiveness over fear. Power over paralysis.

That's the rebellion. That's how you reclaim yourself.

Exercise: Alchemising Your Trauma

Take out your pen lovely, as we reflect and journal on the following:

- What is the most traumatic event you've lived through?
  Don't rush this. Honour your response. Give it space.

- What strength, wisdom, or resilience did this experience give you?
  If you can't see it yet, that's okay—just ask the question. Let it sit.

- What emotions, beliefs, or patterns are you still carrying from this event?
  Be radically honest. There's no shame—just awareness.

- Who do you need to forgive in order to feel free?
  It might be someone else. It might be yourself. Maybe both.

- What would your life look like if you stopped
  identifying with the trauma?
  *What if your story isn't what happened to you—but what
  you chose to create from it?*

- What is your next step in healing or integrating this
  experience?
  A ritual, a conversation, a letting go, a bold reclaiming?

And now, my love, we are ready to walk the path of
Honesty.

Module 2

Honesty

The moment you face yourself, the healing begins.

Your whole world has fallen apart. Your natural inclination is to immediately rebuild.

Hold that thought.

If you go now, you'll just rebuild more of the same.

This is where you need to take a step back, open your eyes, and do some deep work to ensure that when you do recreate, it is with purpose, and absolute clarity – and that you are armed with a full toolkit for success.

Come with me as we meet a whole host of quirky characters who all play a part in your life performance.

You're going to take responsibility, uncover your ingrained patterns and beliefs, examine your weird behaviours, learn to accept change and flow with the ever-moving tide.

5

It *is* My Fault

You can't reclaim your power if you're still pretending it's someone else's fault.

The moment you own your part is the moment your comeback begins.

Here's the deep truth no one wants to admit: most chaos is *not* random.

It's a reckoning. It shows us where things weren't quite right in the first place. When systems fail, when relationships crack, when businesses fold, it's not just bad luck. It's feedback from the universe, a flashing red light saying: *'Look here. Something's not aligned.'*

When we're in the depths of despair, it's so bloody hard to see that, to notice that it's all kinda happening on purpose. Sometimes what we need is a learned companion to point this out. So, I'm going to introduce you to your first 'alter ego' friend who will be joining this mission.

Meet The Truth Fairy.

She's a feisty little truth-talking glitter-bomb who will slap you round the face when she finds you sitting in a pool of denial. She's sassier than Mary Poppins, sharper than your inner critic, and covered in more glitter than a Saturday night in Soho. Part spirit guide, part disruptor — she's armed with a crowbar in one hand, and a mirror in the other. She doesn't come with a wand. She comes with clarity.

She's *YOUR* Truth Fairy.

She's not here to stroke your hair while you spiral. She's here to kick down the doors of denial with her pointy-toed boots of purposefulness! And sprinkle glitter on your growth.

She's bold, she's blunt, and she's got absolutely no time for your excuses. But she does have time for your success.

You'll feel her kick in the moments you're tempted to shrink. You'll hear her sass when you try to blame someone else. And you'll thank her — eventually — when she whispers:

'It's your mess, babe. Now clean it up.'

So, if you start squirming through these next chapters, don't worry. That's her work. She's not here to make it comfortable.

She's here to make it *TRUE!*

Embrace her and welcome her on your tour bus to transition!

Ready? All aboard!

If we want to escape the loop of destruction; we have to look honestly at what caused the chaos—not just who triggered it.

What patterns were playing out? What wasn't working? What did we choose to ignore, override, or sweep under the rug in favour of being busy, productive, or just liked?

Failure is never failure unless we refuse to learn from it. Every collapse carries a seed of insight—but only if we're willing to dig through the rubble and get real. The longer we resist that honesty, the more we invite the collapse to repeat itself—until we learn! This is where you stop dodging that mirror. No more blaming the market, the team, the timing.

Don your helmet and your mouth guard and get ready to do 10 rounds with the hard truth in spangly boots!

Welcome to your reckoning.

It's time to get with the programme, *ma cherie.*

If you've reached this chapter, chances are that you're serious and ready to get honest with yourself. You're done pretending it's everyone else's fault. You're done pointing fingers. You're ready to look in that mirror and say it:

It IS my fault.

Before your ego throws a tantrum, or you fall into a pit of darkness, let's clarify what that means. It doesn't mean that you're personally to blame for every shit thing that's ever happened to you.

It means that you are choosing to stop handing your power away. It means that you are shamelessly claiming your ability to respond — to rise, to repair, to redirect.

Victimhood is easy. It gives you something to talk about. It keeps you safe. It gathers sympathy. But it doesn't build anything. And it certainly doesn't set you free.

To design a life of purpose, peace and power, we have to stop playing the blame game. It's time to own our choices, our patterns, our energy, our outcomes.

When fraud hit my business, it would have been easy to say, 'That's not my fault.' But the truth is I hired that person. I missed the signs. I had a part in the story.

When we got slammed by COVID and had to pivot fast, we made mistakes. I could have blamed the world. But I didn't. I reviewed, refined, and got back in the ring.

I've been burned by consultants, advisors, and banks. I've had people let me down, lie to me, betray me, promise one thing, and deliver another. But if I stay in the story of what they did, I miss the deeper wisdom.

What did I ignore? Where was my boundary weak? Where was I outsourcing my own knowing?

You're not a puppet. You're the creator.

You don't need to be perfect to take full ownership of your life.

You just need to decide *I am the one who gets to shape what happens next.*

There are generally two types of people in the world: the Winners and the Whingers. This might sound harsh, but it's true.

Winners - put themselves out there. On life's stage. Under the spotlight. They have a goal that they want to achieve. They will make a positive difference to the world, for themselves and for humankind. They have big ideas, and they go for it.

- If and when they falter and fail, no matter the conditions, they look inside for the solution.

- They practice self-awareness and they seek to improve their own method.

- They don't look to blame circumstances or other people.

- They take full accountability and responsibility.

- Yes, they might seek redress for negligence which has directly contributed to a situation, but they will do this with calm fairness and professionalism – certainly not with an entourage of vengeance and pity.

- They do not harbour feelings of blame, resentment, or anger towards those who may have 'wronged them'.

The most powerful realisation that you can have is that whatever is in your life now, you have either asked for or tolerated. It is nobody else's 'fault'. You are indeed the master of your own destiny.

Don't get me wrong, it's not always easy to admit that, especially when it has caused a collapse. And even the most steadfast Winners can slip into a Whinge from time to time.

That includes me. But those who know their ego well enough, (eventually) accept responsibility, which undoubtedly leads to clarity and solution finding.

If I were to blame all of the things that affected our business, on the third parties involved, then I would relinquish control over my whole life. I would be denying my own bumpy road!

The truth is that as the business owner, I have overarching responsibility for all of it.

So, after I'd had a whingy rant, I put my big girl pants on, and I took responsibility.

You see, the common denominator here is me. It's exactly the same in your life or your business. The common denominator is YOU. Once you accept that and roll with it? That's the game changer.

Here's the lesson: it's not about the challenge itself. It's about how you process it. What you do about it. If you can take accountability no matter what the circumstances, then you will always come out a Winner!

Whingers, on the other hand, are often unable to take this leap into accountability.

You will know these people. Everything in their life 'happens' to them.

When you ask them politely how they are, you receive a war and peace response often starting with the list of health issues, followed by some doom and gloom from the news, and topped off by a tale of some awful creature who has wronged them in some way.

I am not talking about vulnerable people here, who are likely to have a list of genuine ailments and woes.

I am referring to fully functioning adults in their prime, who just can't seem to see the good in anything. Nothing is their fault.

- They did the diet that worked wonders for everybody else, but for them it failed – the diet was a load of rubbish - it wasn't their fault.

- They were set a reasonable task at work, but they missed the deadline, their boss was too demanding – it wasn't their fault.

- When they enrol you into their pity party, and you try to help, they come up with a problem for every solution you offer them.

- They complain every time they eat out, go on holiday, or even just venture to the shops. Everything is a let-down. None of it is their fault.

- They lack the self-awareness to realise that they are creating their own suffering by putting too much importance on that which is really not important.

If you are a whinger, my goodness, you need to wake up. Give yourself a massive shake, a kick up the bum, a slap round the face. Whatever you need to do. You need to sit down in front of the mirror. Stare yourself in the eye. And declare out loud 'It *IS* my fault.'

You can't keep blaming your circumstances, past and present, on others. After all, your driving instructor isn't to blame if you go out alone and you crash your car.

You must decide to be accountable, in control, in charge of your own outcomes, then you become a winner too!

It's like people who complain that nobody loves them, or nobody wants to spend time with them. It's always the other persons fault for not giving enough of their time. If the blamer looked inside, they would realise that perhaps they are not making themselves very loveable?

If you want to be loved, you have to make yourself loveable, right?

Here's the next lesson: If you go out into the world wearing your invisible coat of armour, expecting a battle, because the whole world is against you and everybody is wrong - you are setting your subconscious up for a fight. And of course, it then delivers the circumstance that ignites that behaviour in you. Drop the shield, and say sorry – you'll be amazed when all of your troubles just turn and walk away.

The answer is always within you.

If you are reading this now, and you have just had a moment of profound realisation that you might be a whinger. It isn't too late to change. It's time to do some self-work.

This is an opportunity to dig deep, go through whatever is grating on you. Write it out. Pull out the beliefs, analyse the patterns.

What are you doing to create these unwanted events in your life? Read on as throughout this module you'll learn how to identify and disarm these dysfunctional patterns.

Is it time to turn your hatred into love? Your fear into gratitude?

Stop trolling, and instead take heed of the positive leaders, the ones who journey through pain without complaining! The ones who thank the lord for the blessings in the struggles. The ones who *just Fricking Do It!*

You can change!

You deserve success too!

Everybody does.

Play full out and push past the 'little mind' who cares what others think and say. Use adversity and convert it into immense power to propel yourself forwards.

That, my dear, is how you freaking succeed. That is how you join The Winners!

Take all of that negative energy, transmute it into love, load up a cannon with it and shoot yourself up into the stratosphere! Stay true to yourself and freaking fly!

I'll meet you on the moon!

Now that is power.

Exercise

So, what's it gonna be? A victim of the world? Or a bona fide, accountable force to be reckoned with? The Winning bus is leaving. Answer these questions to get on:

- Where in my life am I still waiting for someone else to change?

- What is one thing I've blamed others for that I now choose to take full ownership of?

- What decision am I now ready to take full responsibility for—regardless of the outcome?

"Well done, darling. You took your first slap like a champ. But don't get comfy—what's coming next is going to hit even harder. I'll be right here with my glitter cannon."
— The Truth Fairy

6

Peanuts

Who are you trying to impress?

You've just looked in the mirror and admitted it: *you were part of the chaos.* You've claimed your power back. Bravo.

But now comes the real sting:
you weren't the only one in there.

Somebody else was in there too.

And you opened the door to let them in!

Hmmm… recognise any of these traits?
Being a Shrinking Violet.
People Pleasing.
Playing small.

Now here's another truth bomb - The biggest challenges in life, and therefore the greatest learnings, are always going to stem from people. In fact, not really the people themselves, it's the way that you react to them.

*"Oh, hello again, darling. Still trying to win Best Supporting
Role in someone else's movie? Let me be clear: people-pleasing is
just manipulation dressed in polite shoes.*

*You're not helping—you're hoping. Hoping they'll like you.
Hoping they won't leave. Hoping they'll finally say, "good job"
and give you a pat on the head.*

*That's not kindness, babe. That's captivity. If someone can't
handle your brilliance, they're not your people. So, stop shrinking
yourself into snack-size. Full-size, or nothing at all."*
— The Truth Fairy

Now before you fall back into the comfort blanket of
underperformance and over giving—let's talk about how
we hand over our power… one polite little peanut at a time.

The Peanut Principle

I'm going to dedicate this analogy to my long-time bestie,
Linsey, who is a true peanut. She is a nutty nut. For real!

Her nuttiness has stood beside mine for 30+ years,
holding me to account and reminding me of exactly who I
am, every time I have needed to hear it. So, thank you to my
truly moreish friend who I can always depend on for a dose
of comforting wisdom. She is a wise nut indeed!

Right, enough of the mush, it's time for the big reveal!
Da da daaaaah! Drum roll, please…

You my dear, are a peanut!

Yep, that's right, a peanut. And I'll tell you why.

Some people can take you or leave you. You either haven't registered as much of a 'thing' in their universe or you might be a bit 'meh' to them! How effing rude! Ok, ok, don't start getting offended already!

Others will find you utterly delicious – especially when smothered in chocolate, wink wink. They'll devour you at every opportunity, and in any form—a crowded Snickers, or an intense peanut butter moment. They just adore you. Can't get enough of you. They scoop you out of the pot by the handful, as often as time allows!

On the opposite end of the scale, there are those who find you abhorrently distasteful. They don't like your texture, can't stand your smell, and detest your bittersweet flavour. You give them the ick. They vocalise this frequently.

There's a minority of the population who are actually severely allergic to you. Hanging out with you might even cause a fatal reaction. They carry defences, to neutralise you at any moment. They are intensely fearful, and go out of their way to avoid you at all costs. You are not good for them!

Fancy that eh? Get involved and they will damage your reputation!

Wow, isn't it amazing how one lowly nut can incite such an array of responses?!

Despite all of this, the humble peanut doesn't go on a power trip when it realises its popularity.

Neither does it get a complex when a stranger it has never met before declares they can't stand peanuts.

It doesn't blame itself either, when somebody faints in its presence.

After all, it's just a nut. Its only concern is its nutty self. And it rightly does not try to change the opinions of others.

So, here's a question…

Are you in charge of you?

Ok, you might think that's an insane question, and that you are completely in charge of your own self.

You're an independent human being, right?

Or are you?

The one thing that controls your actions is how you feel.

How you feel determines how you act, and therefore how you present to the world, and of course, how successful you are at achieving your desired results.

Feelings, or emotions, are actually the catalyst to EVERYTHING that you do. If you're not feeling it, you won't do it. So, answer this one with utmost honesty. Do you decide how you feel? Or do you let other people do that for you?

It's actually an *incredibly* difficult question to answer, because of course we all want to be deemed fit to control ourselves. But unfortunately, for most, the majority of the time, we are simply not.

Our heads have a tendency to turn into fluffy love-spun candyfloss if somebody chats us up.

Or we seethe with fury if somebody badmouths us.

In either one of these instances, the moment those words leave the other person's lips, we are taken from our contented buddha-esque plane of calm. And we suddenly morph into vengeful twits, rose-tinted nitwits or worse – sad little stagnant sausages. *Imagine!*

None of these alter egos are who we set out to be. They are the direct result of us allowing 'other people' to determine our feelings—and lord knows what actions these volatile characters might take next.

I propose that the most important life skill we can master, is to be unaffected by the good or bad opinion of others,[11] a mantra that the great Deepak Chopra has poured into my mind for many years.

Of course, this fits right in with the Rebellion Life Principles – after all, the true Rebel doesn't, and shouldn't, give a hooting toot what other people think of them.

If you can nail this, you have nailed life. But I'm not gonna lie—it is probably going to take some work.

Enter: The Haters

First of all, you must learn to be completely at peace with the fact that some people won't like you. There is nothing you can do about it. You just don't float their boat, you're not their cuppa tea, you 'grate on them'. Your success pisses them right off. They can't handle your positivity.

Get over it. Deal with it. Strike them off your Christmas card list and thank them for saving you the price of a stamp. Leave them be. What they think about you, is none of your business. Tough, but true. Mind your own business and stop giving a hooting toot.

Renounce your self-image right now. It is ok for people to not like you. It's for them to decide, so let them. Don't try smothering yourself in chocolate to appeal to their tastes – just walk away.

Some of these people will be passive in your life, they will stay on the side lines and mumble. Others will stake a claim on your happiness. But guess what? They can only take it *if you allow it!*

I speak from experience here. I used to do just that. This is
one of the biggest reality checks of my life.

Back in 2023, I thought that I had pretty much
mastered life and my emotions. I had immersed myself
in mindfulness work over the previous years. I had come
through COVID 19, armed with an all-new shiny coat of
resilience. So, there I was like Billy Big Balls, ready for
anything. I was cool as a cucumber, and pretty sure that I
could be a 'casual observer' in my life.

Not so.

I was tested with a huge bombshell, which shook me to
my core.

I totally fell off my magic carpet, and was sucked
straight back into my 7-year-old self again, in a hostile
playground, facing a sea of bullies. I just wanted the ground
to swallow me up. And for a while there, I let it.

What happened was horrific at the time. My heart
was broken, in the cruellest manner, by somebody who I
thought was a friend.

It really was the stuff of playgrounds. They set up a
'witch hunt' against me, and enrolled others, many who
I'd also thought of as friends, into the bullying campaign.
Slanderous untruths, hateful fearmongering. Really
despicable behaviour. But I cared too much – so much that
it broke my heart.

This person had actually asked me to be a godmother to her child. She wrote gushing posts saying how thankful she was to me, and how proud she was to be our friend.

But meanwhile, behind closed doors, she was stabbing me in the back, infecting the ears of those who would listen, and cooking up a master plan to try and destroy not only my business, but that of my mentees too.

I retreated, and I spent the next few months in a dark space of self-reflection, intermittent depression and illness. I let it get to me. Big time. I felt so violated.

These haters, these blamers, these victims just cannot admit that they are responsible for their situation. They are hell-bent on bringing you down because they're not being as successful as they want to be. They see that you're doing well, and they hate it.

Hate is the most poisonous feeling. When you're feeling hate, you're making your own blood boil. You're attacking your own body and mind and making yourself poorly. It's destructive on all levels.

I've heard so many tales lately of good people being attacked by haters.

It really is such a shame. But let it be their shame, not yours. When you lead from the front, you're always going to have people behind you stabbing you in the back.

I've been called everything which I wouldn't repeat by one particularly complimentary chappy. Such hateful slurs without a thought for the harm that words like these could do. It shook me up at the time, but what I really felt was pity for him.

Let's spare a moment for those lost souls swimming in a sea of hatred and venom, slowly poisoning themselves with contempt.

Nevertheless, I did allow them to penetrate my aura. To infiltrate my bubble of happiness. I fell weak with exhaustion, and I allowed them to shape my world, which was a very sad world, for a period of time.

I completely retreated. I came off socials. I stopped mentoring. I didn't go out. I woke up every morning with an ache in my heart wishing that the day would be over before it had even begun, I contemplated my very reason for existence. I wondered if I could ever be myself again.

And then—I remembered who I am.

I recalled that actually, until I got into property, I didn't know who the frick any of these people were. I realised I was allowing my life to be controlled by two disillusioned, narcissistic ninkynonks and some hangers on.

I realised I had spent so much of my life giving my time and my caring heart to those who didn't value me or my friendship, they had just enrolled me out of convenience, to assist on their journey.

In that moment, my soul was awakened—and the switch happened. I started to see, to really see.

I didn't want them in my control centre anymore.

How to Handle Professional Bullies

Like an irritating pimple, it's best to just leave them be – seriously. It's so tempting to want to squeeze the little bugger, but don't. You'll end up with a bright red crater and puss all over your face. Perhaps even a scar. Leave them and they'll retreat soon enough, back into the beautiful skin of life. And don't worry about your reputation. Anyone observing your face can see it's just an angry little spot. Don't draw attention to it. Don't give it the focus. Save yourself the drama.

"You don't squeeze it. You don't feed it. You don't try to reason with it. You just stop poking it and let it dry up and fall off."
– The Truth Fairy

Cheerleaders

In those moments of despair, my true friends, my cheerleaders, stepped forwards—in the hundreds! They held me up, safe from the snakes. They had told me to put my dancing shoes back on and just freaking dance.

So I did, wearily at first. But eventually I found my wings, as they lifted me on an undercurrent of love that was so strong, it smashed all negativity into insignificance.

I have always massively loved and appreciated my friends, but this love grew tenfold, and I really started to ponder the significance of it all.

You see, there is no greater testament to the character of a person, than the strength of their real tribe.

I realised then, that I was something to be celebrated. I was loved. I was valued. I was needed. I had a purpose. And that is the most special and valuable realisation that anybody could have.

Suddenly, my loneliness disappeared and unveiled the huge amount of support I had. The trolls became tiny and insignificant, and my loved ones, my real tribe, my chosen indispensable crew – well, they grew!

They were larger than life, they were present. I became overcome with love. A deep sense of belonging enveloped me. It was the biggest spiritual awakening of my life.

Without my haters, who I now look on with such appreciation for this momentous aligning of my soul, I would have perhaps never come to this realisation.

It was such a beautiful and profound new level of understanding, and I had never experienced it before.

Now, I can honestly say that I am at peace with the haters. I have so much love and strength, I don't need to give any of my focus to those who don't want or don't need it.

But what of the haters? People like this will surely, upon their death bed, regret their ways, won't they?

Or will they?

Do they even realise the harm they are doing to themselves?

If ever they were to glimpse an ounce of self-awareness and change their ways, they could transform their lives.

They could stop needlessly striving to push people out of their way. They could stop seeing competition and collaborate instead. They could lose that awful feeling of envy and replace it with pride.

Hate destroys the person who carries it. When you hate on somebody, when you think of them and your blood boils —guess whose blood you're boiling?

They need to drop the hate and learn to love.

I gave up on hate many years ago. I simply don't contain hate. Ever.

I send a prayer of healing and love to my 'haters' every night. If only they could glimpse their own light.

The Tribe

The Tribe can be wonderful. Your heart-centred support system. Your cheerleaders, besties, and loved ones. This Tribe is a group of empowered beings who champion each other and urge each other to succeed, who share ideas, wisdom, and strategies, without requiring anything in return.

A real Tribe will listen without judgement, they'll open their hearts when you open yours, they'll cherish your friendship, they'll stay true and loyal.

Furthermore, this Tribe doesn't measure or judge anybody on their 'success.'

But, the tribe can also be dysfunctional.

When the Tribe Turns

T - Too many

R - Relatives

I - Interfering

B - Blindly, without

E - Experience

As a Tribe member, you will have to accept disapproval from friends and family at times. Your own will must be stronger than the doubt that arises from your 'Tribe'. This is often the most difficult set of 'other people's' opinions you will have to negate. Because you love and respect the person who is 'blessing' you with their 'wisdom'.

But you see, when you decide to step out of the 'tribe' and do something a bit different – like buggering off to travel around the world or starting up a new business, you realise how much other people do try to interfere with your plans.

It's funny how, when you declare your decision for personal betterment, everybody seems to have an expert opinion (usually fear-based) on something they know nothing about.

They are fearing your unknown. They are creating a big ball of imaginary doubt. They are also scared of you leaving them behind – safety in numbers, right? And so, they will attempt to hold you back from your break for freedom, by terrifying the living daylights out of you with their anecdotes of *'my cousin's friend's ex-boyfriend did that and… disaster!'*

I remember when I told my Grandma – God bless her, that I was going to Africa on Safari.

Her response? 'Oooh you be careful, they do that female circumcision there! They'll have your clitoris off!'

Needless to say, I went, had a marvellous time, and came back fully intact!

More shockingly, my Gran then went on to ask me what a clitoris actually is – a question that I was absolutely dumbfounded to be asked by a woman who had birthed eight kids! Flipping heck!

The moral of the story is that we don't listen to the tribe of naysayers, the victims, the opposers and objectors who want you to stay in the 'comfort zone', just like they did. Do not be pulled back into the bucket by the crabs. Take no heed of the opinions of those with zero experience on your chosen path.

Their intentions might be in the right place. Their fear is genuine, and they're acting from what they think is love. But please don't let them put you off your dreams. It's only their own insecurities.

Nothing like a tribe to put you off your stride. You're better than that! You know your values; you know your truth. Crack on!

The Heart Sink Test

To set yourself up for success, you should be super choosy about who you surround yourself with, think about who you really want to share energy with.

I have a rule, it is a strict rule that I put in place after my heart-breaking moment with 'pretend friend' up there!

You see, I realised that she was that friend who, when she called, and I saw her name flash up on the phone, would incite a 'heart-sink' reaction.

Some people do that, don't they? With this friend, I never knew if she was gonna say something nice, have a right go at me, or launch into a hate fest about some other poor soul – it was usually option 3, which always made me exceptionally uncomfortable. Bitchin ain't my bag!

No wonder that my heart sank when she rang. So that's my trick, and I suggest you use it wisely – when the phone rings, if your heart sinks, that's not your friend! Dump them now before you get hurt, like I did – unless of course it's your mother-in-law, in which case you might have to tolerate this one!

But if it's a 'friend', I'm telling you now – they are not!

If I'd have used my intuition and this trick to size her up, I'd have never let this person get so close and would have saved myself a whole lot of grief! But this is a lesson I needed to learn.

On the flip side, when a true friend calls, or you even think of them, your heart will warm, and you'll smile from ear to ear.

True Tribe, True Love – Mixed Nuts

These are the beings to keep in your life. Your true friends. Your long-time lovely nutty nuts!

Dedicate your life and gift your time to the ones who matter.

Nurture your relationships with loved ones, appreciate your friends, be kind to colleagues and inspire the best in your employees.

Join soul-nourishing tribes and accept their support. Avoid the gossipy, cliquey, judgy ones, and certainly don't hang your worth on anybody else's opinion of you – let the nut-adverse teach you this lesson, as our biggest irritants are also our best teachers. Learn to keep them at arm's length. Your soul is bigger than any of this. Be the casual observer and let others do as they will, but without affecting you.

Fill your joyful inner circle with the ones who make you smile.

NO Ninkynonks, NO Negative Nellies, NO Nitwits!!! Just Pure Wonderfulness!!!

THE chosen few

THE indispensable crew

THE Rebellion Tribe

So, crack on, Rebel. Be the nut you were born to be. Full-size, flavour-loaded, unapologetically you. And if anyone's allergic to your deliciousness? Well, that's their bloody problem!

Exercise: The Cost of People Pleasing

Pens at the ready…

- Where in my life am I currently saying yes when I mean no?
  (Get specific — name the person, the situation, the fear behind the yes.)

- What parts of myself do I dim, edit, or hide to be more palatable to others?
  (Think appearance, opinions, boundaries, energy.)

- Who taught me that being "liked" was more important than being free?
  (Dig deep — this is where your conditioning lives.)

- What does it cost me — emotionally, energetically, financially — to keep pleasing?
  (Write the real price. Put numbers or time to it if you can.)

- What would it feel like to stop apologising for who I really am?

Come on now little peanut, that was a tough task. But shedding those who will only spit you out anyway, is empowering as hell.

The next chapter will bring your smile back.

Let's go.

7

Robots

And perfectly silly humans

I don't know, humans! We're all a bit nutty, aren't we?

I mean, if we're not under the influence of other people's opinions, we're demonstrating all sorts of insanely weird behaviours, some of which seem to take us in the exact opposite direction to our goals.

Because—now it's time to face the truth—*you haven't ever really been in control!*

What if most of what you do—what you say, how you respond, the way you sabotage, the choices you make— hasn't really been you at all?

What if it's been your programming?

If you can sit with this—if you can be honest about what's been controlling you—you can change everything.

And you will.

It's not just about what we do. It's about what drives what we do.

This is where we take a look under the hood—at the unconscious patterns and inherited beliefs that keep us stuck in the same frustrating places.

You might think you're choosing freely, but often, your behaviours are simply echoes of old programming.

Childhood conditioning. Cultural messaging. Trauma responses.

This next chapter will examine how we sometimes run our lives on autopilot—like puppets in our own show. But don't worry—this isn't about shame. It's about *awareness*. Once you're aware, you can rewire everything.

Robot

Imagine if you'd invested in a fancy, fandangled, new house robot. The stuff of movies. A thoroughly helpful handy person in metallic form. Top of the range, with all the bells and whistles, and the promise of an easier life for yourself and your family.

Stay with me here and picture yourself in your living room, with said robot, let's call her Nancy for the sake of the story. Picture Johnny 5 from the 1986 film, *Short*

Circuit,[12] (Google him, if you're not as ancient as me!) – in a frock.

You fancy a nice cuppa tea. So, you ask Nancy, as her first task, to go and make you one. Simples, right?

Not an over-complicated first task?

Nancy has been programmed already with a road map of your house, she has all of the information on how to get to the kitchen, how to open the door, where to find the tea bags, how to operate the kettle, or the Quooker tap, if you're posh!

She has it all there in her robotic brain, the location of the fridge, and the milk. The instructions are very clear, to meticulously fine detail, about how to make a cup of Yorkshire tea to your exacting standards.

So off Nancy goes, best foot forward, very proactively, towards the kitchen door. She has a mission, and she's chosen to accept it! Nancy is the latest generation of house robots, and she is sure of her ability. This menial task will be a piece of cake for her.

But as soon as she leaves the living room, *da da da* (dramatic disaster sound) – she encounters the vacuum cleaner, who is loitering in a dark corner under the stairs. The vacuum cleaner makes a slightly condescending joke about Nancy's ability to perform her tea-making task.

For a brief moment, Nancy's internal circuits flicker as she hesitates; her programme has been slightly interrupted with this new data! She doesn't know what to do, she's confused. Should she still proceed? She dithers and procrastinates. She wasn't prepared for this!

An inkling of doubt replaces her unwavering programming—an echo of the inner critic we all know too well.

She feels silly going back, but she's fearful of going forwards too. Eventually she blocks out the noise of the vacuum cleaner as she hears you shouting to ask if she's ok.

Still reeling from the earlier jolt, Nancy takes a deep, digital breath….

And she proceeds into the kitchen. She starts to boil the kettle, but just then a cheeky little toaster starts sniggering at her. Now Nancy becomes very self-conscious, as the toaster asks, "Who are you, and what are you doing here?"

Nancy now has full blown Imposter Syndrome. *Aaaaghhh!*

For a split second, the kitchen falls silent as Nancy's confidence wavers.

She is overcome with anxiety. If she could breathe, she'd be hyperventilating. It's then, just when she's at her weakest moment, that the bloody kettle pipes up with, 'Are you sure she wants tea? She normally has coffee!'

'Oh, for f*cks sake!' screams Nancy in her technical tones, overwhelmed by the barrage of negative voices.

Now she doesn't know what the heck she's doing. With crushing self-doubt chipping away at her resolve, she's totally lost control and faith in her mission and her ability to complete it.

Her malfunction button goes into overdrive. Nancy's system falters further and she retreats to go and hide under the stairs with the meany vacuum cleaner.

In that dim, unlit corner, Nancy feels sad and unfulfilled.

For goodness' sake! What would you think?

'Bloody daft blinking robot!' is exactly what you'd think.

Of course, this would never happen to your technical companion in real life.

But it does happen with us humans, all too often.

We learn new skills—reprogramming our minds with fresh data and information.

We set off on our mission, all guns blazing and cock sure. Until either our own self-talk sneaks in to knock us off track, or haters, tribes, random people on social media who you've never even met before (in fact they might not even be real) all step in to help you confirm those self-doubts and scupper your plans for world domination.

Now who's the daft blinking robot? You! Me! It's the human condition!

We're so intelligent that we're ridiculously good at self-sabotage.

"Well, well, well, what do we have here? Another darling do-gooder with a dream… hiding under the stairs again, are we?

Look at you—so bloody brilliant, but still letting your old wiring call the shots.

Let me make this very sparkly clear: You are not broken. You're programmed. There's a difference.

Your robot isn't faulty—it's just following a shit script.

But Love, guess what? You're the coder now. Not your mum. Not your old boss. Not society. You.

So if you're tired of rebooting into sabotage and shame— maybe it's time you wrote a new line of code.

One that doesn't start with: "I'm not good enough."

Now straighten that crown, override the drama, and march your shiny inner Nancy back into the light!"
— The Truth Fairy

You see, my darlings, the point of this story is that it doesn't matter how many courses you do on a particular subject. It doesn't matter how well-learned you are, if you don't know yourself.

Mastering your subconscious patterns and becoming aware of your sabotage triggers are the keys to success.

To achieve blissful fulfilment, you need to do both – learn the skill and learn *yourself*.

Because there's nothing so frustrating as knowing that you buggered yourself over, let yourself down, and didn't follow up on your promise.

Whatever that promise was—setting up a business, transforming your body, giving up alcohol. All of it! You will just default back into your incapable 'comfort but not actually comfortable' zone if you don't rewire yourself for success.

We shall delve more deeply into this in the following chapters. But for now, ponder on this story for a while.

Exercise

Just think about how many times in the past 12 months you've given up on a mission due to procrastination, self-doubt, the opinions of others, or lack of confidence.

- How many times have you gone to hide under the stairs, and allowed your own dreams to falter under the weight of doubt and criticism?

- Where would you be now if you hadn't let those blockers hold you back?

- Where are you running on old programming?

- What were you taught to believe about money, success, or yourself that still influences you today?

- What new belief or pattern would serve the person you are becoming?

There's some food for thought!

Right then, Prepare to expose your own faulty wires next as we adventure into the programmes and patterns that unsuspectingly control your every move.

Come on now, Nancy – out from under the stairs! We have work to do!

8

Beliefs and Patterning

"Whether you think you can,
or you think you can't – you're right."[13]
– Henry Ford

Robots would never behave like humans, with our doubts, neuroticism, and ability to convert any molehill into Mount Kilimanjaro!

We launch ourselves into each day, full of gumption and gung-ho. Determined to succeed.

And by the end of the day, we're stuffing a packet of Jaffa Cakes into our faces, to paste over the pain of our failures.

So why do we do it?

Behind every robotic action is a *belief*. A story you've accepted as truth. A piece of programming picked up somewhere between your first breath and your first

burnout. These beliefs aren't facts. They're illusions. And if
we want to break the loop, we have to rewire the code.

This is where it gets raw.

So take a breath. We're not judging—we're observing.
This chapter is about seeing clearly who, or what, has been
running the show.

*"Darling, let's just get one thing straight: that voice in your head
that says, "I'm not enough"? That was never yours.*

*But it's running your entire bloody operating system like
some snide little backseat driver.*

*You didn't choose it—but now you get to **change it.***

*You don't have to keep wearing beliefs like hand-me-down
knickers just because someone else left them in your drawer.*

Delete. Rewrite. Reclaim."
— The Truth Fairy

Mindset and consciousness really are the key to sustained
success in all areas of life. The moment you start noticing
your patterns, you reclaim your power.

This isn't just about wealth—it's about every area of
your life. Relationships, health, self-worth—these are all
shaped by subconscious programming. Once you identify
the script, you can rewrite it.

And that, my darling, is where true freedom begins.

Beliefs

If you were raised in a home where money was tight, you might believe: 'I don't deserve money.'

If you were praised for being helpful and polite, you might believe: 'My worth comes from pleasing others.'

If you were criticised for being too loud, too wild, or too emotional, you might believe: 'I'm too much.'

These beliefs become the blueprint of your behaviour.

They don't scream—they whisper. And they become your decisions, your boundaries (or lack of), your relationship choices, your risk tolerance, your voice.

You start a business, but you don't charge enough—because deep down, you believe you're not worth it. You stay in a dead-end relationship—because you believe love always has to hurt.

It's not logical. It's *emotional coding*.

And it's time to rewrite it.

Once you become aware of a belief, it stops being your ruler and starts being your responsibility. You question it. Replace it. Upgrade it.

This is where power begins.

Despite ourselves and our ridiculous human habits, we do have the power to create a life that is bewilderingly surreal.

So now we go deeper!

Patterning

Patterning was a word I'd not heard since my knit one, pearl one days in the 1980's when my Grandmama taught me how to create my own absolutely shocking woollen garments.

It was 2019, and as Sean and I sat there on the conference room floor at the Bloomsbury Hotel in London, listening to a high pitched, and actually quite bonkers South African, the legend who is Ryan Pinnick, I knew when he said 'Patterning'[14] that he was not referencing my long-forgotten foray into knitwear production!

What the blinking hell was he on about? Patterning workshop? Sounded like something that goes on in the church hall in Midsomer, not something *pour moi*?

Wrong! It was absolutely something *pour moi*!

And it's totally something *pour toi*, too!

Patterning is the process of tracing back unconscious habits, triggers, and emotional reactions to their root cause—and identifying the series of events that inevitably follows, so you can write them off for good.

This Patterning Workshop[14] was probably the most powerful self-awareness deep dive exploration that I'd ever encountered.

It was just a few weeks earlier that we'd bumped into this chirpy chappy at a property event.

To hear someone talk about mindset at a property conference was certainly not what my husband Sean and I were expecting, yet it was his unique approach that inspired us to sign up.

So off we went to do 'Patterning'[14]—which, I must hasten to add, is not merely identifying one's beliefs. It's much more involved than that.

It's about analysing the unwanted results, the perceived catastrophes and disasters experienced throughout one's life.

The shocking moment is when you realise that you have repeated said pattern throughout your life, multiple times over – pissing on the notion that you were acting with free will and confirming the fact that you have been a puppet, controlled by a fear-driven 7-year-old. Jeez, that's tough to swallow. Which is why I don't recommend venturing into patterning on your own.

Patterning[14] awareness is a carefully cultured art form. To get the most out of it, it's best to work with a Patterning coach.[14] I have held sessions with my business mentees, and it can ignite some pretty brutal emotions, so be careful—make sure you're in safe hands. But get it right, and this is probably the biggest 'awakening' you will ever have.

Not only has this work provided us with deep awareness around how to structure and manage ourselves better to create success, it also helped us to develop that level of self-awareness where we can identify and pick out re-attachments to old habits and dysfunctional traits.

It's also given us the ability to develop our intuition and foresight, to such a degree that we can make better decisions. Including the decision to admit when it's going tits up!

Now, more than ever, we understand that consciousness is the key to sustained success in all areas of life. We have utter certainty in what we want to achieve and know without a doubt that we will get there.

Now, don't get me wrong, Sean and I are still students – we always will be. Never be cocky enough to assume you know everything – if you do, that's the moment you stop growing.

Self-mastery is a life-long challenge, and even if you start pulling out your patterns at the age of 16, you'll still be at it when you're 70. The difference is, you'll have a wonderfully aware life throughout that time. You'll see with the lights on.

Conscious Explorations

I suppose that, from the outside, Sean and I may seem an unlikely pair of property moguls.

But my husband and I, unassuming as we may seem, possess a certain level of eccentricity that enabled us to step out of the expected – and into the realms of the unbounded.

Eccentricity like this may be partially soul-grown, but it's also a collaborative cultivation of the deep work that we've done over the years. The reprogramming, rewiring and patterning. The multiple journeys that we've taken into the unknown.

We've faced our 'real' selves head on more intensely than Atreyu from *The NeverEnding Story*.[6] We've never once professed to know everything. Quite the opposite. We relish every lesson, every critique, every slap in the face as an opportunity to go deeper and to learn. And that, I believe, is what sets us apart.

Your internal programme is absolutely key to the results that you see in your life. EVERYTHING you do is predetermined by your inbuilt script. What many don't realise is that your programme was written from the beliefs you formed as a child, mostly before the age of 7.

These beliefs have then been re-validated throughout childhood, so they become fully imprinted on your subconscious mind.

Your subconscious mind *IS* quite simply the most powerful hypnotist in the world. You can declare every morning that you're never eating chocolate again, but if chocolate was something your Mumma popped in your mouth every time you were upset, you'll find yourself uncontrollably hunting down chocolate like a burglar in your own kitchen, when you feel the deprivation.

Your 7-year-old inner child is screaming at you that chocolate is comfort, and you need the fricking stuff to survive this world!

So unless you learn how to tap into your unconscious mind, you will continue to live out your limiting childhood beliefs – the ones that tell you you're not good enough, there's no money, you can't do this and you can't do that, chocolate makes you feel good. All that utter nonk.

Let me ask you a question, when did you last update your phone? I bet it's not more than 6 months ago.

Next question, when did you last update your subconscious mind? Have you ever updated your subconscious mind?

No?

'Nuff said!

This isn't just about discovering patterns. This is about taking back control of your life. You're about to see how your subconscious has been running the show—and by the time we're done, you'll have the power to rewire it.

So, although it would be irresponsible of me to lead you through a Patterning[14] workshop, without 1-2-1 support, we can do an exercise to identify some of your limiting beliefs – and after all, beliefs are the coals which fuel the patterns – so let's analyse our childhood 'wealth stories' together.

Exercise: Beliefs - Identifying Your Wealth Story

I'll tell you my story if you tell me yours!

Write out the story of your history with money, and pick it apart.

Can you see how these stories could cause a small child to form a belief?

Don't worry, I'll be with you every step of the way. First, I'll walk you through mine.

The beginning – a girl like me and a boy like him

So, how did it come to be, that a girl like me and a boy like him made it to where we are?

In short – Sean and I were both born and raised in single parent households on some of the roughest council estates in Leeds – we had our fair share of reality checks forced upon us. It was certainly a gritty awakening into this life.

We fought with siblings and local gangs, whilst our worn-down mothers worked day and night to put food on the table.

Luxury was a custard cream biscuit; a meal out was a crab stick and sandwich in the working men's club up the road.

We both had glimpses into the worlds of 'rich' people. We could see their success but were not a part of it.

I had witnessed my father go bankrupt three times and each time, survive. He took some major hits, but he got back up each time – resilient and unfazed.

So, what did we learn?

- Life is tough.

- There isn't enough money.

- There is a rich life, but we don't really belong in it.

- You have to work REALLY HARD to get money.

- Money = Power.

- Keep going and survive no matter what.

- You have to fight for your life.

- Scarcity is all around.

I knew, as soon as we entered the property world, that we might make a lot of money. And I was also very aware, given our upbringings that we would likely have some negative beliefs around wealth that could hold us back.

The goal was to unveil our wealth blockers. But the result was far deeper than that. It actually allowed us to foster a deep understanding of each other, our relationship, and our little quirks too – which was so powerful that we suddenly became tolerant of our differences. For the first time, we understood ourselves and each other.

What started out as a practice to protect our wealth, opened us up to a whole world of inner transformation that we never expected.

Where we started to discover our true value.

Now, it's over to you!

Step 1: Write Your Story

Write out your earliest memories around money, success, and struggle. What was said about money in your house growing up? Was it scarce? Was it a source of stress? Or was it an empowering tool?

Step 2: Identify the Core Beliefs

Now, pick apart your story. What beliefs did your childhood experiences ingrain in you?

Step 3: Identify Your Programming

How do these beliefs show up in your adult life?

- Do you self-sabotage in ways that mirror your childhood programming?

- Have you ever felt like you're stuck in a loop, where no matter what you do, the same things keep happening?

Now, let's go deeper into how to break these beliefs.

Step 4: Recognise the Lie

Look at the beliefs that you identified, and ask yourself:

- Where did this come from?
- Is it true?
- Do I want to keep it?

Behind every false belief, there is an untruth.

Take a good look at the beliefs that are not helping you, and identify the lie to disarm the false belief.

Example, Untruth: *Chocolate is love.*

Example, Truth: *My mother loved me very much. She showed this the only way she knew how: through chocolate. But chocolate is sugar laden, unhealthy and will make me un-love myself more. She didn't know any better at the time. I can appreciate my mother's love now by nourishing myself with beautiful, healthy foods.*

Step 5: Reframe It

Find a new belief to replace the old one. For example:

- Old belief: 'You have to work REALLY HARD to make money.'
- New belief: 'Money flows to me through inspired action and aligned decisions.'

Prompt: Write your old belief and replace it with a new, empowering one. Affirm it multiple times a day.

Step 6: Take Conscious Action

- Catch yourself in the moment when an old belief pops up.

- Pause and choose a new action aligned with your new affirmation.

Prompt: Write down three situations in your life where you felt financially, emotionally, or mentally blocked. Can you see a common belief at the root?

Now, no need to wing it with this one, my love. For a FREE Beliefs Exercise Template, which includes a full version of my story and Sean's that highlights every ingrained belief, head over to www.rebellion-life.com/beliefsexercise.

You've done the hardest part—you've opened your eyes.

The next step is up to you. Are you ready to rewrite? Because your new story is waiting.

I know, it's not for the faint-hearted. This work is deep. It's hard.

But come on now, wipe away the tears, take my hand and let's do a badass strut together into the next phase where we bring your magnificence out!

Hop back on the tour bus, grab Nancy and your glitter-punching winged companion. We're about to pick up Shirley, for a full-on road trip to the Transformation State!

9

Shirley – Your Story

The band is in formation. And now it's time to change your whole damn sound.

You've unearthed your beliefs. You've faced your old programming. You've started to understand how your subconscious shapes your story—and how that story becomes your reality.

Now comes the wild part.

Because here's a truth that most people won't tell you:

your chaos didn't just happen to you.

Your chaos came from the stories you told about who you were, what you deserved, and what was possible.

The collapse? The self-sabotage? The repeated patterns?

They didn't show up to destroy you.

They showed up to reveal your authorship.

And that means admitting something very few people are ever brave enough to admit:

'I unconsciously manifested all of it.'

That's not weakness.

That's power.

That's **honesty.**

So, are you ready to look at the identity you've been wearing like an old outfit?

Let's go meet Shirley!

Who is Shirley? She's a key player in this star-studded, glitter-spangled band of growth. You, Nancy, The Truth Fairy and Shirley! All aboard the tour bus.

Shirley is in fact, a beautiful stuffed leopard who was acquired at a flea market in France.

Shirley is rather large, and was not particularly welcomed by Sean, who didn't want to have a huge great cat taking up space in the back of the car, all the way from Bourgogne.

However, after much protesting from a certain little bird, Shirley won the day. She made the 700-mile trip, which thrilled our little bird, despite the 17-hour berating rant from our Seany (although not quite on the same level as when I smuggled a huge piece of extremely stinky Epoisse cheese on a later journey!).

And Shirley, in all her greatness, is now a fully-fledged member of the McDermott household. She's been living with us, mostly lolloping on our sofa and looking glamorous, for the past 12 years.

What on earth has this got to do with your story, you might be wondering?

More than you might think, actually!

Shirley is a leopard, and there's a famous saying that: 'a leopard cannot change its spots'.

In Shirley's case, this is entirely true. Shirley is a stuffed leopard and does not have the ability to change her dyed-on plush spots.

But you, my dear, well, you can definitely change your spots – because you are real. And a real leopard really can change her spots. She can do that the moment she realises that she was the one who painted them on herself.

Ponder on that one for a little while. Profound, huh?

You see, we all write our own stories: we paint them onto our outer shells, and we display them to the world. They are the representation of what goes on in our inner world. And our 'spots' are both the impression that we leave on other people, AND (this is the important bit) the mark that we leave on our subconscious minds.

These impressions ALL come from OUR story. This is the story that you tell others on repeat about yourself, your life, and your luck – or lack of it. This story, with every recital, is reaffirmed and further indented into your subconscious.

This is the catalyst for manifestation. So, we have indeed painted on our own spots, and we are the ONLY person (or leopard) who can change that.

Sure, we can convince ourselves that the world drew our spots on for us, or that our parents did it, that it is not 'our fault', and that there's nothing that we can do about it. But that doesn't serve us. It might seem easier to go for the denial option. Because, as previously discussed, most humans are not wired to accept blame, take responsibility, or be accountable.

BUT if we can admit the truth - then the power is completely within our hands. We are the ones holding the paintbrush, the pen, or the crayon. And we do have the power to change our spots.

Of course, most people never come to this realisation. They remain trapped in an unconscious state—never feeling in control, always being pushed back, held away from their dream life. Repressed. Suppressed. Unfulfilled. Stuck under the illusion of some 'outer force' controlling them — without realising that the force is actually themselves!

The universe will only act in alignment with your requirements. And as long as you are repeating a tale of woe, and bad luck, that is all you are going to get more of!

Your subconscious listens more intently to your words than anyone else ever will. It is extremely impressionable. Like a small child – your inner child. It will believe and enact whatever you tell it.

It's very much like the Genie in *Aladdin*.[15] With each wish, the Genie will take control of your being, ensuring that you play out your command, as sure as a puppet would act out a play.

If you're forever complaining that you're 'completely skint' to anybody who'll listen, banging on about the traumas and wrong doings at the hands of others who 'put' you in this place, then your mini-Genie will hear that you are skint. And clearly you want to be skint as you keep saying it.

And guess what the result will be?

It's like saying to a child 'right then, we're going to be cowboys today!' That child will become fully invested in the vision, they will believe themselves to be a real cowboy, and they will act it out in glorious detail. Next time you're out shopping, and they spot a cowboy suit in the fancy dress department; they'll do everything in their power to acquire that outfit. They will stop at nothing, relentlessly pushing until you give in and buy it. You are powerless as they are having a screaming tantrum on the floor.

You see – they *need* it! It's their only focus. They must have it so they can further validate the belief that they are, indeed, a cowboy. Your subconscious mind behaves in exactly the same way. Once you have planted that seed, you are powerless against it, until you stop planting the wrong fricking seeds!

Furthermore, as you continue to tell your tale to every willing victim, until their ears bleed, you are also cementing their impression of you. People do judge. Not always intentionally. But people do make sense of their own worlds and their own self, by comparing their world to yours.

So, every experience they have of you, forms a more detailed impression. If they think that you're always skint, they're either going to feel sorry for you and also spread the word to others that you are troubled financially.

Or, they are going to avoid you like the plague, in case you want to borrow a tenner.

An enlightened friend might also steer clear, as they find your energy is off kilter with theirs, and they prefer to focus on the good in the world.

In any case, all of these results are going to make you feel bad, and poorer still.

As for your own Genie, well, apart from the fact that the poor bugger can't get away from you — they are a small, obedient child, they will not doubt or question you. They'll take every word as an instruction. So, they are going to do all that they can to carry out your request. Ensuring that your hearing is piqued when bad financial advice comes your way.

Ensuring you are distracted when a great opportunity arises. Pushing your 'suspicion' button when somebody offers a lifeline and keeping you in a state of anxiety so that solutions just don't land.

This is the law of attraction at its best and worst – and whether you believe it or not, thoughts trigger emotions, emotions shape behaviours, and behaviours create results — good or bad. It all begins with a single thought.

Do you think that Richard Branson got to where he is by crying a poor tale to all and sundry? Did he - *buggery*. He decided where he was going, and he wrote his story accordingly.[16]

Think and Grow Rich by Napoleon Hill is perhaps the most famous self-development book on the planet.[17] EVERY wealth guru references this book, because they have read it and been influenced by it and the thousands of publications that are born from it.

It's no coincidence that the richest, happiest and most fulfilled people you know believe 100% in this undeniable universal law. Yet the 'woo-woo poo-pooers' are often stuck in their own poverty traps.

Unable to see the good that exists around them. Most of them are self-proclaimed victims who constantly look to blame others and allow the world to 'happen' to them.

Powerless pawns in their own lives. It's sad, really. I've encountered my fair share of them and it's incredibly difficult to help them awaken and see the true picture.

They hang on so entirely to their story, they make up whole scenarios to explain their lack of results, which never holds them accountable for their own life. And this is purely and simply because they spend their lives reaffirming to themselves and others how 'unfair' life is.

Is this you?

Let's be honest— it's most of us sometimes. We are only human and we're all still learning, myself included. I have my moments!

The difference is that many of us will catch ourselves being pulled into a negative rant, even if it's in our heads (they're the worst as they can go on for days!,) but we can spot the toxicity and pull back. This is how we learn and how we grow.

However, those who don't believe that they are the masters of their own misfortune will struggle to ever come out of their self-bated trap, as they just can't see it. They will continue to write their sad tales and repel all the good things in life – if only they would open those blinkered eyes.

Remember the Winners and the Whingers? This is exactly why you don't want to hang long-term in the whinging camp.

I have no shame in admitting that I've spent some time sitting in 'camp a la whinge'. Like I say, nobody is completely ego-immune.

If you've had a run of challenges, eventually your mental strength can wear down, you let your guard slip and dip into victim mode.

As you know, Sean and I have had a few bouts of chaos. And at times it's been difficult not to slip down that slope.

I remember writing a letter to our finance broker to document the challenges for a lender, and my goodness it was like fricking War and Peace. Thousands of words of whinge! One big, long, victimous moan! It was empowering to face my own whingewaffle – as it highlighted just how dysfunctional and unhelpful my thoughts and words were.

So, if somebody like me, who has been hailed as 'far too positive and too woo-woo' by some of the victims in my life, can also be dragged into that realm, then you need to beware.

You can halt your demise the second that you admit that you hold the paintbrush, and you did indeed paint your own spots.

"Oh hello, leopard. Still pretending your spots are permanent? Let me remind you, darling: you painted those spots, remember? Every self-deprecating comment. Every humble-bragged trauma tale. Every single time you downplayed your greatness so others wouldn't feel uncomfortable.

You made the mark. And guess what? You can unmake it.

So, here's a little wand-wave of wisdom:

Your identity isn't fixed. It's fashioned.

It can evolve. Expand. Explode. Glitter-bomb itself into something entirely new.

Babe, if you're gonna rewrite the story—make it one that makes the whole bloody jungle sit up and purr."
— The Truth Fairy

The first step, as always, is self-awareness.

Think back to the stories you have told over the years. In fact, what is the last story that you told a friend about yourself? You might have thought you were just letting off steam when you declared that you are sick to death of your husband, and you'd be better off without him.

Be careful what you wish for!

Or did you go on a rant about the price of everything in the supermarket? Validating the belief that you are struggling financially.

Did you complain about the rich getting richer? Repelling a rich life.

Did you mention that you feel destined to be alone forever? Sealing your fate as a spinster.

Whatever it was, to your Genie, it was an order from the universal catalogue of fate!

Write it down. Write down all of the stories that you have told yourself, and others. The stories that you tell yourself can be even more damaging.

'I'm not good enough.'

'I hate my body.'

'I'm scared of those people.'

'I don't trust myself with money.'

It's time to delve deep and pick your thoughts apart. See how incredibly counter-productive they are by analysing your own words. Then, we can start to change them, together.

The good news? You're never stuck in one camp. The moment you shift your perspective, you can pack up your things and move in with the Winners!

Exercise

So, here's your challenge: Pick up that pen. That paintbrush. Take a moment of honest reflection. Face your spots—all of them.

Write them out. Draw them out. See them for what they are. And then—choose. Will you keep them? Or will you rewrite your masterpiece?

So, come on, you glorious velvety leopard, you! Let's go deeper. Where did those spots come from? How were they painted in the first place? Because once you see that—you can start to change the design.

Answer the following questions:

- What identity have I been performing that no longer fits who I am becoming?

- Whose voice do I still hear when I try to step outside that version of me?

- If I were to rewrite the story of me from scratch—what would I keep, and what would I let go of?

- Where in my life am I still editing myself for someone else's comfort?

- What would I dare to do next if I believed I was safe to evolve?

You are not fixed. You never were.

You were never meant to be boxed in by one version of yourself, one identity, one neatly labelled story that made everyone else feel comfortable.

You're allowed to outgrow your patterns.

You're allowed to reinvent.

You're allowed to strip it all back, keep the parts that still feel true—and lovingly discard the rest.

Shirley was the mirror.

Changeling, the next chapter, is the metamorphosis.

So now, my love—let's stop apologising for our evolution and start stepping into it with power.

Let's crack open the next layer.

Let's change, darling.

10

Changeling

It changes every day. Every day, the tide delivers a different story.

You've done the unthinkable. You've faced yourself. You've dismantled the blame, the people-pleasing, the outdated beliefs, the patterns you inherited but never asked for.

You've looked in the mirror and admitted: *'this version of me has expired.'* And now, my love, this is where honesty blooms into something sacred. This is where change becomes your medicine, your rebellion, your art.

Myth: Consistency is key.

This is true to a certain degree, because of course you must diligently show up, as your best self, and put in a consistent amount of effort. And I'm absolutely one for persistence and pushing through tough times.

But, I also appreciate that flogging a dead horse is a sure-fire way to frustration and loss! So, if Chaos has come waltzing in through your door – throwing all that you once knew out of the window – take it as a cue that something needs to change.

After all, repeating the same behaviours, and expecting a different result is the definition of madness, right?

Rigidity can be stifling, and if there's one thing the last few years has taught me, it's that adaptability is key to survival.

Covid for one, has proven that many businesses who buried their heads in the sand, or stood firm against change, ultimately collapsed. Those who rode on the crest of the wave and adapted their businesses to meet new market demand survived.

Just as a business must evolve to thrive, so too, must our personal narratives shift with the winds of change.

So, what happens if you have poured your heart and soul into a relationship or a business, and it doesn't work? It just flops? Falls flat on its face?

Or what if life is a resounding success, but then something completely beyond your control swoops in and floors you?

These are probably the two questions that put most people off from starting a new relationship or setting up their own enterprise in the first instance.

But the rebellious ones out there know that it is in moments like these that we find the treasure. Opportunities always spring from adversity.

Don't be a failure, be a changeling. For every failure is really a lesson. And every lesson brings us nearer to the truth. If something ain't working, switch it around. Take what was right, remove the elements that didn't work out, morph it into something else entirely.

It's highly likely that if, for example, your business is failing, there is either an inherent disconnect with your values, or your customers' needs are not being entirely met.

If you can accept this and move on, you are one step ahead of most.

If you can appreciate the value of the 'failed' business and transmute that failure into magnificence, you are a true leader.

Constant and consistent – these are the notions that some of us want to strive for. With our 'settled relationships,' our '9 to 5 jobs,' and our 'daily routines'. But they are just notions.

Not many of us mere humans ever actually keep these consistencies in check for a lifetime.

After all, no matter the field – business or life, change is undeniable.

In reality (whatever that is), there is little constant. Indeed, the only constant is the knowledge of being, of pure divinity.

The rest of us know little, but strive anyway, against the tide, desperately trying to keep the world still, with fear in our hearts and doubts in our minds, making our own lives into a misfortunate struggle against what is in fact, inevitable.

Because to deny change is to stifle one's own spirit.

That deep frustration that we feel at the end of a fruitlessly dull day, is due to a lack of change. Due to a lack of diversity. You didn't make a difference today, so you feel awkward, and restless. Like a weakened shoot that didn't manage to break through the soil into the daylight. That unrealised bloom is the very epitome of dissatisfaction. Poisoned potentiality.

You see, we are artistic creatures of immense creativity. We flourish and thrive with change. We are changelings and we must move with the tide.

It's time to surrender to the flow. Sometimes the most empowering thing is to let yourself drift on the unpredictable and boundless waves.

See what beautiful cove you might end up in, and with whom you might arrive. Let be and let your soul be.

Arrive unprepared, but use your resourcefulness. Make your own way, seek the tools which are already laid out for you. For the universe provides everything that you need – if only you'd open your eyes, drop your preconceptions, and just build.

Accept the beauty of transformation.

As a child, I was forever followed by a swarm of ladybirds.

I'd diligently collect them in a Stork margarine tub. Then, I would bring the colourfully entertaining community of miniature scarlet dancers into my otherwise uninspiring bedroom. I'd observe them with glee! Mesmerised by their interactions. I'd handle them with intense care – very conscious of their fragility.

For a fleeting moment they brought all the wonderment of a circus into our concrete-panel council house, with its threadbare carpets and blown vinyl walls. My limitless childish imagination would convert those grey-rendered walls into a palatial residence every time my dotty-spotted friends came to visit.

Then, I'd release them back into the hedgerow. A day or two later, they'd leave, on the tail of the wind.

At all times of year, be it early winter, late spring or mid-autumn, those delightful little dears now gather on the front door of our house. Beguiling my girls as they once did me with their interesting ways, and their delicate features.

They've followed me through the years. They sit quietly, waiting to surprise me as I step outside at the break of dawn—or when I return home from a long, intense day.

In any case, and despite our life-long relationship, they still make me gasp with absolute joy, as my dependable winged comrades seem to arrive on the most unexpected of days.

Not the type of day that one would usually associate with the swarming of mystical insects – not a warm and inviting day. No. They are mystical indeed. As they are often there on an icy morning, a blustery evening or during a monsoon-like storm. My special breed of ultra-resilient ladybugs.

And then there are the burglar versions – at times when every window in the house is firmly shut, yet there they are, bold and brazen and tip-tapping their tiny toes along the insides of the sash frames, admiring themselves on my dressing table, or flaunting their lucid rouge waistcoats against the glass-like ebony lid of the baby-grand piano in the lounge.

But how do they do it? Those beautiful but uninvited house guests never fail to astound me with their dedication to provide such wonderment – as the miniscule Houdinis magically appear without even a puff of smoke. And for an audience of just me.

On the advice of a psychic, I looked into the meaning of the spirit animal 'ladybird,' and I was thrilled to realise that they are a symbolism of transformation and positive change. Of course, this made complete sense. Transformation, for me, seems to be my constant state.

As soon as I have reached a place of comfort, or achieved a specific goal, I seem to be whisked out of my seat and flung back up into the air to face more of the chaos, the tests and painful challenges that have conspired throughout my life to prevent 'stagnation' in any form.

And my micro-messengers are here to remind me of my own resilience, of my aptitude for change and transformation, of the number of times that I've retreated into my chrysalis and emerged as a slightly better, slightly bolder, and slightly more confident version of my previous self.

They illuminate my own spiritual journey and give me the faith that keeps me strong and fearless when I am walking yet another unknown and unlit path.

They remind me just how wonderful transformation is. And just as transformation is revealed in the mundane, so it is inevitable in business.

In many ways, I am still the child with the margarine tub. Innocent and none the wiser to the ways of the world, with much to learn and much to do. With a loving heart and a desire to be loved.

And in other ways, I'm as wise as the trees and as old as the seas, with the indentations of many lives etched into my very essence. You could call it halfway to learning. But is it really? Or do we un-learn as we 'adult' in this life?

I think the latter is true a lot of the time!

One thing that has always mithered me about adults is that question we feel we must ask to all children: 'What do you want to be when you grow up?'

It really is the strangest question. It's a question from an un-learned place, and we all ask it! It took me a while of catching myself, to prevent those words from leaving my lips and invading my daughters' friends' ears when they were small.

It gives that child the notion that they must be one thing for the rest of their lives, and they must decide it now. How strange that is. And how incredibly tedious to pop yourself in a box for the whole of adulthood.

Let's not expose them to the notion that they are just one thing.

I used to love watching *Mr. Ben*.[18] I loved *Mr. Ben*[18] because, in every episode, he would put on a suit and take on a completely different persona/career.

One week, he was an astronaut, and the next, a cowboy. And nobody ever judged him for being indecisive, nobody ever came and asked him what he wanted to 'be'.

Be inspired, be limitless, and be everything that you could ever imagine being. Be it all. And be proud of that. Be the change.

Maybe, for a little while, I would like to be a ladybird, with all the freedom of the air, the colours of a rainbow and the magical capabilities of a wizard!

So, the whole point of this whimsical tale, is really to open your eyes to the fact that there is no shame in admitting that your previous way is no longer THE way.

Adapt your business to your needs. Leave your damaging or just mundane relationship. Don't give a hooting toot about what others think! They may judge you for back-tracking, side-stepping or swerving that which you might have previously endorsed.

Or maybe they won't, because just maybe they're too busy worrying about what you think of them!

Embrace change when the time is right.

Change is a natural part of life, and without it we would all wither and die. This is your life, this is YOU.

And whether you've hit a financial crisis, or you're just not feeling the level of fulfilment that you'd hoped for, it's quite alright to swap your cowboy hat for an astronaut suit, or your vineyard for a ladybird farm. You know yourself and your business more than anybody.

So don't be too proud to admit that it's not going to plan. Delve deeply into your resourcefulness and make another one. That's what we do – the Rebellious changelings out there.

There's absolutely no shame in taking a purposeful pivot!

Since my health scare 'awakening,' Sean and I decided to increase our fulfilment by changing our business from offering holiday homes, to focusing more on events and parties.

After my beautiful friend reminded me that I am 'born to party and to flounce', it made me question why I am not doing more of that.

And yes, initially I wondered what people might think. But I soon pulled myself back into check as it has absolutely no relevance whatsoever what other people may or may not think.

The fact is that most people won't even notice. They are most definitely too busy wondering what you and others might be thinking about them and their business – funny creatures, aren't we?

You really must value your own happiness over the opinions of others.

If change is the right thing to do, and by that, I mean, if change will enhance your business and enchant your life, then change is good, so embrace it.

Caveat: please don't use this advice as an excuse to just give in or give up on your true purpose, or your life's dream because things are getting tough.

Every business will face challenges. There will be moments of financial crisis and unwanted stress. But as long as you can see a light at the end of the tunnel and you have a plan to get there, keep going.

The time to change is when something feels really wrong. When you're only still going because you are frightened of the opinions of others, and you don't want to be perceived to be an ass.

Or when the universe takes the decision out of your hands and collapses your world.

Exercise

Let's walk that path together. Ask yourself:

- What change have I been resisting?

- What do I yearn for that I'm not yet doing or living?

"This isn't the end. This is the pre-show.

They may call it indecisive, flaky, chaotic, but just laugh! Because you were never meant to stay the same. You're not a filing cabinet—you're a bloody unicorn! A glitter storm in human form!

Change isn't failure. It's evolution. It's the universe remixing your destiny until the beat finally fits your soul.

Now go on, changeling. Rebuild. Rewrite. Revolt.

Cue the confetti. Crank the rebel anthem. We roll at dawn."

— The Truth Fairy

Module 3

Awakening

Open your eyes my lovely – look deeply into your world.

You've ridden through the gut punches of the two most difficult modules.

You've done the self-reflection and the deep work.

Now, it's time for the fun to commence!

You're right on the arc of the CHAOS acronym, and it's so perfectly timed as you are also at the arc of your personal journey from Collapse to Success—because this is exactly where the pain turns into lessons.

The moment of awakening is like being reborn again – opening your eyes for the first time in the big, wide, wondrous world. And *blooming heck*, it's exciting!

It's the transition from dependence on a host
to the realisation that you have been breathing yourself all along.

It's the point when you suddenly realise your own potentiality and you see the world for what it truly is – a playground of your own creations.

Everything looks brighter and more purposeful. The winds of change become the carriers of dreams.

So next up, prepare to gain not just awareness, but some seriously badass skills that will set you up for a life 'on purpose'.

This module is layered to perfection, like a joyous trifle.

The base layer peels back your eyelids and exposes the obvious truths – in Hallucinations, and the What HIFs.

Then you've got a super fruity mid-layer that will slap your light bulbs on harder than a tequila slammer, as you jump to attention in Motivation and Sparks.

And finally, your dream topping is the custard of Manifestation, with some seriously whipped Energy stealing the show and cementing your route to success.

This trifle isn't just any trifle – and no, it's not a bloody Marks and Spencer's Trifle either, you daft bat! It's a Trifle of Truths and Tools – because once you know and master this stuff, you'll wonder how you ever lived without it.

Great whopping spoon at the ready—prepare to fill
your boots!

Yum, yum, tuck in love.

11

Hallucinations

All is not what it seems!

Before you get too excited, I'm sorry to tell you that this chapter, 'Hallucinations', is not at all related to psychedelic adventures. Not that there's anything wrong with a bit of spangle-tastic exploration!

But, whilst psychedelic journeys might open the doors to perception *a' la* Aldous Huxley,[19] the everyday hallucinations I'm talking about here slam them firmly shut—keeping us locked in patterns we don't even realise we've created.

This chapter is about the *un-fun* hallucinations.

Of the most deceptive kind.

These hallucinations are the doom-tinted spectacles of mediocrity, carefully crafted from misguided beliefs—so you can be damn sure they will omit all routes to success.

They fall into two categories.

1. Your own home-grown hallucinations – false views of reality which stem from your story.

2. Other people's hallucinations, which they insist on stirring into your already confuzzled pot of perception soup!

Either of these can sweep you right off your success path and dump you in the ditch of dissatisfaction!

So, why do we have them?

First of all, let's make one thing clear. *Nothing that you can see with your eyes is real.* Quantum science has proven that. Everything that exists in this dimension is a cloud of energy: these clouds vibrate at different frequencies, and our limited brain interprets the apparitions into solid objects.

So, life as we know it, is one big hallucination.

You'd have to have been living under a rock for the last decade, my love, if you've not grasped this one yet, so I'm not going to bore you with the science – but Google it and spend some time listening to Dr Joe Dispenza[20] if you're still part of the 'so solid crew'.

Now then, when everything is a cloud of potentiality just waiting for interpretation, each person perceives that cloud differently. It's like abstract art. Nobody really *understands* it. So, we make it fit our pre-conceived ideas. It becomes relevant to our circumstance.

Our eyes literally wear the lenses of our own beliefs. And most of what we *could* see with our lying eyes[21] (singing *The Eagles'* track in my head right now!) gets filtered out.

So, you are seeing a unique and tiny fraction of 'reality'.

How utterly fricking weird is that?

But true. Psychologists call it confirmation bias.[22] Neuroscientists call it your RAS—the Reticular Activating System[23] in your brain that literally filters what you notice. I just call it hallucinations, because to me, that's exactly what they are.

Have you ever been to look at new cars, and noticed one particular model that you really fancy? Suddenly, you start seeing them everywhere. You'd never even noticed one on the road before! Now, they're as common as Vera Duckworth![24]

This is no coincidence. It's your mind filtering those energetic apparitions according to its expectations.

And this is exactly where those naughty hallucinations come in.

Remember that absolute load of nonk you made up about yourself when you were a whipper snapper?

The Story you repeat—to yourself and all other poor unsuspecting souls.

It doesn't just control what you think.

It pre-determines what you *see* too.

For instance, you have a belief that people whisper about you when you're in crowds (because a rotten little snot bag once had a snigger at your expense on a school trip)—and although you are now 35, *EVERY* time you walk into a crowded bar, you are convinced there's a mean-looking person, who is whispering nasties about you.

The reality of the situation is that they probably haven't even noticed you!

If they have, they *might* be telling their mates that they think you're hot.

See how your hallucination can completely misconstrue an otherwise perfectly pleasant interaction, Doomzilla?

But as I said at the beginning of this chapter, these little devils come in two guises. Your own, and other peoples'. So, how do we get blindsided by other peoples' hallucinations?

Like this: you tell your friend, Peter, that you're thinking of attending a networking event. They warn you against it—they went last week. It was really cliquey. There was a sea of unwelcoming faces.

This was of course Peter's own hallucination, but nevertheless, you don't go because they thoroughly validated your fear of hostile strangers.

A few days later, you bump into Jay, an old work colleague, who *did* go to the networking event. It was ace, everyone was so friendly, and since attending and shmoozing like a pro, several big opportunities have opened up for him—including a new investor.

You are left feeling like a prize tit for riding on somebody else's catastrophe cart.

Maybe Jay has already read this book!

Do you see how two different people can have opposing perceptions of the same situation?

Just remember, that whatever you are imprinting with your 'woe is me' life story, your 7-year-old ego will display on the pixels of your life, complete with jaw-dropping cinematic effects, ensuring you play out your patterns like *Groundhog Day*. [25]

Furthermore, other people will enrol you into their hallucinations as they work just as hard to validate their stories, too.

Every 7-year-old ego craves validation and recognition. They fear being wrong. So, they will stop at nothing to be right.

Relentless little tricksters—masters of hallucination, without the DMT!

This is why we need to parent ourselves, interrupt the programme, and rewrite the story to suit our lives now.

What story are you still running on loop? And more importantly—what would you rather see showing up in your life instead?

If you don't want to be it, then don't flipping see it with your story, *ma cherie!*

These hallucinations—the ones born from childhood wounds, tangled beliefs, and other people's unhealed projections—they've shaped your entire life like shadows cast on the wall of a cave.

But now, you've seen the light.

Awakening is choosing to stop living on autopilot, to stop seeing through a pre-drawn life, and to start visioning perfection.

You're not here to keep playing out the same old story.

Erase the outdated VCR and start projecting brilliance. Put the doom specs down (and the shroom specs too). It's time to wear the 24k gold blingtastic lunettes to light your way.

You are the seer, now see!

Exercise

Alright my love, time to whip out the pen and answer me this:

- What hallucination have I been living in?
  (*A belief or story I've been mistaking for truth.*)

- Where have I adopted someone else's version of reality—and made it my own?

- If I saw myself and the world clearly—with no filters, projections or fear—what would be possible?

So let's venture into that realm – where your wildest dreams become your reality.

It's time to open your toolbox and prepare to fill it with the good stuff.

12

The What HIFs

Hindsight, Insight, and Foresight

You've cleared the fog. You've started to see how much of your past was shaped by fear, by projection, by perception dressed up as truth.

Now? It's time to get intentional.

Because when you can see clearly, the next question becomes: *where are you heading?*

On the great map of life, every direction is fraught with decisions. Each crossroad has a barrier – and you need a tool to ensure you're not about to head into the quagmire. So here it is. Every time I face one of life's great quandaries, I pull out the What HIFs.

The What HIFs are a rebel's roadmap for decision-making. A way to walk forward with clarity—often gained from chaos.

Let's start with that age-old question… *What If?*

- *What if I ask them out and they say no?*

- *What if I start that business and it fails?*

- *What if I'm not good enough?*

- *What if the market crashes?*

- *What If?…*

I've heard this question *so* many times in my life, especially as a mentor. My usual response is: *But what if all your dreams come true and you live happily ever after?*

That's where the *What HIFs* come in. They replace the *What Ifs*.

The *What HIFs* method helps you make informed, confident decisions. When you master it, you stop being paralysed by *What Ifs* and start moving forward with clarity. You can see behind, analyse the present, and plan for the future.

But before we get into the detail, I'd like to dedicate this chapter to my husband, Sean. As a typical Yorkshireman, he loves to put H's where they don't usually belong, and yet completely omit them where they do. A true rebel! A typical sentence from Sean might be:

"Ello love! I 'erd there was a hotter on the riverbank last week." ('Hotter' being 'otter'.)

It's almost an independent language of wayward H's!

For this chapter, I have borrowed Sean's knack of misplacing an H and added it to my *What If* to bring you a powerful lesson!

Let's delve into the *What HIFs*.

Fear vs. Strategy

The question '*What if*' arises from a fear of the unknown. Essentially, you are questioning the validity or viability of an idea because it's something you've never ventured into before. Your ego is churning out a deluge of risk factors, listing every possible way you might make an absolute tit of yourself in the process.

Now, this is actually a good thing: it encourages a necessary risk assessment and ample due diligence on the subject, problem, or venture at hand. But instead of letting *What Ifs* paralyse you, we are going to replace them with the *What HIFs*—Hindsight, Insight, and Foresight.

Let's be honest – when you've just come through a monumental collapse, your confidence may be a wee bit shaken. And you might find doubt creeping in. But, with the *What HIFs* in your toolkit, you've nothing to worry about. Master this lesson, and you can get back in the driving seat of your life with confidence.

The What HIFs in Action

Let's use the example of buying a car.

Imagine you've always had a Toyota (mid-range but reliable). But for years, you've fancied yourself in a Merc. You've had a promotion at work, you yearn for a driving holiday on the Italian Riviera, and you'd really love to swank along in style!

So, off you toddle to the Mercedes showroom. You're immediately bamboozled by the fancy spiel of the salesperson. The car looks glorious, and there's a fairly good offer on it. But you do the sensible thing—you don't sign up on the day. Instead, you say you want to sleep on it.

You drive home in a dream, already resenting the mediocrity of your Toyota. But as soon as you settle down, the *What Ifs* start to creep in:

- *What if* it's unreliable? It could be a diva car!

- *What if* the parts cost a fortune?

- *What if* another model comes out that's even better?

- *What if* it guzzles petrol like your Auntie Sheila on a bottomless brunch?

- *What if* your friends think you're a twat in a fancy car?

- *What if* you lose your job?

- *What if, what if, what if?*

It's so funny how we can dream about something for years on end, but when we are actually faced with realising that dream, the *What Ifs* pop up to scupper it—to 'keep us safe' and grounded. Hmmm.

The best thing to do in this, or any other 'What If' situation is to replace the *What Ifs* with *What HIFs*. And this is where your research begins.

Hindsight, Insight, Foresight

Let's break it down with our car example. For this lesson let's take the first question:

1. What if it's unreliable? It could be a diva car!

Hindsight

Hindsight is about looking at past experiences—either your own, or others'.

Now, with car purchases, this is easy really. With t'interweb at your fingertips, you can research multiple review sites and find out from the hindsight of others whether it's a reliable model.

Let's imagine, that in this instance, you find that most reviews are good, but a few mention issues with Apple

CarPlay connectivity. At first, you might think, *'Not a big deal.'*

But, upon deeper thought, you realise that CarPlay is your satellite navigation and in-car entertainment. A glitchy system could diminish your entire luxury experience. Thank goodness for hindsight, right?

Yes, of course, but it doesn't mean that you have to pivot and stick in your comfort zone Toyota forever. You just need to come up with the insight from the hindsight. And then use that insight, to form foresight, so you can take action with an advantage.

Insight

Now that you have hindsight, the next step is gaining insight—how can you use this knowledge to your advantage?

The insight here is that you've discovered the issue *before* buying. Now you've got negotiation power—and protection before you commit.

Foresight

Now that you have hindsight (problem identified) and insight (negotiation leverage), you can apply foresight— your action plan.

Your foresight tells you that the first thing you do when test-driving your new car is test Apple CarPlay. If it works perfectly, great! If not, you either negotiate a better deal or reconsider the purchase.

This is quite a simple scenario for the sake of demonstrating the method. But it's the same with anything you're considering getting into—whether it's buying property, starting a business, going on a date, or even moving abroad. Whatever the quandary, use the What HIFs.

Applying the What HIFs to Life

Hindsight – Learn from the past

The best place to gain hindsight is from your own past experience. So cast your mind back to any similar situations. How did you react? What were the outcomes? What did you like or dislike? What insights can you extract?

If you lack personal hindsight, seek it from someone else who has been there before—as long as it's realistic and doesn't involve their hallucinations! For example, if you're starting a new business, it's advisable to get a mentor who has been there and worn the T-shirt.

My mentees pay for my hindsight—the expensive lessons I've learned, the intense challenges I've ridden—so they don't have to make the same mistakes. In the property development world in particular, hindsight can be a very valuable commodity. Each lesson allows me to pay it down—so they gain the hindsight for a fraction of the cost, and a much lower risk.

Insight – Extract the lessons

Insight is the *realisation* that comes from hindsight. The flash of inspiration, the sneaky peeky, the big reveal or the epiphany that comes from Hindsight. It's the *oh* moment.

Like, when you start talking to a guy online who wants to take you on a date. Your hindsight reminds you of the last date: it went really well or, so you thought, a little too well—you got thoroughly snogged and a little bit more!

Only to discover, via some Facebook stalking, that he was dating three other women. What a twat!

So, this time, you use your hindsight (previous experience) to gain some insight.

You stalk date numéro deux online *BEFORE* any raunchy snogging occurs. You check him out—he's actually hanging out with his dog, he's got a brand spanking new Merc, and he took his Mumma out for Mother's Day! Lots of ticks! Off you go confidently, armed with some foresight.

Foresight – Take action with confidence

Foresight is about what you do with your newfound knowledge. It's the contract, the guarantee, the boundary, the plan. It's the action you take to move forward without fear.

By this point, you have either aborted mission, or you have made the decision to go for it.

Hindsight, Insight and Foresight are your guiding lights. Use them well and you are triple-sighted.

But, do remember to trust them.

I have seen people fall foul for ignoring warning signs that have come from other people's hindsight – some people only listen to advice if it's what they want to hear. And if they don't hear what they wanted or expected, they make up a story to justify their decision to ignore it.

Then, of course, when it all goes wrong, they will also become a victim. So, don't do that! Listen to hindsight.

Saying that, I have also seen people not go ahead with something fantastic because they've listened to imaginary hindsight (hallucinations) from somebody who has never actually done the thing they want to do.

True hindsight comes from the owner of the Merc, the person who has built the business, the one who followed the diet and lost 5 stone – not from the one who thought about buying the book but talked themselves out of it.

Trust the process, trust yourself, and embrace the future with all three perspectives in play!

Just remember—when in doubt, apply the *What HIFs*... and for God's sake, don't let the *What Ifs* make a mug of you!

Exercise

Pens at the ready again!

- Where in my life am I currently paralysed by the What Ifs?

- What hindsight have I been ignoring—either my own or someone else's?

- What insight do I now see that could guide my next decision?

- What foresight can I create to move forward with clarity and calm?

Right then my love, grab those triple vision specs. You're about to load up a glitter cannon of motivation.

13

Masterful Motivation

Striving vs. Your Big Why

You've mapped the route. You've questioned the fears, decoded the patterns, and peeked through the lens of Hindsight, Insight, and Foresight.

Now comes the fuel.

Because what's the point of a clear path if your engine is going to conk out?

This chapter is where we flip the switch—from Striving to The Big Why. From external applause to internal alignment. From burning out to lit from within.

Self-motivated people will always be just that.

We don't need somebody else to 'heal' us so that we can get on and do something. We just need to take action. We must look inside our own minds and explore our self-awareness until we have that awakening.

Yeah, we might benefit from a coach with the relevant Hindsights, Insights, and Foresights to help navigate the challenges. But, as far as following somebody else's plan is concerned, we don't need it. Our own inner guidance tells us exactly what to do—if we listen.

The times that I have doubted my own intuition and instead taken the advice of 'expert consultants' – knowing full well that they gave me the ick, are the times when it has gone horribly wrong!

A close friend shared his realisation that his own father was always his mentor. When he lost his father, he started looking elsewhere for that guidance. But after getting no further forward, he realised it was inside himself all along.

His father spent years instilling this into him as a boy. But momentarily, following the passing of his father, he forgot his power. He is his father's son, and he is his own self. Together they are bomb-proof, intuitive, God-realised beings, with more get up and go than any self-professed guru.

For most entrepreneurs, having motivation isn't the problem. It's *WHAT KIND* of motivation they have that makes a massive difference to the end result.

Motivation comes in two very different forms, 'The Strive', and 'The Big Why'. One of them will lead you to heaven, and you can guess where the other might take you!

Let's have a closer look…

The Strive

Where does it come from? The Strive? The drive? The thing that captures your mind and whisks you off on another hair-raising adventure every time you dare to sit still for a moment.

It's always been a bloody-minded obsession for me. The kind that keeps you awake at night. The stuff that haunts your dreams… and lives inside your skin, orchestrating your every move towards perceived greatness.

It's certainly not for the faint hearted, and it used to strip me of peace of mind *EVERY SINGLE DAY OF MY LIFE*, with its incessant chattering.

But what is it? And why?

It's your worthlessness.

Wow! That's a shocker, isn't it?

But we all have it.

The reason that some of us strive, with an incessant drive, is because our 7-year-old egos (yep, those guys again!) are trying to prove themselves. They have a deep-rooted association with not feeling good enough, intelligent enough, attractive enough, slim enough, rich enough.

Whatever it is. You do not believe that you are enough.

You can believe this shite your whole life. Or you can nip it in the bud now.

My ego was challenged in a particular way during my formative years, and in my teens/early 20s.

Let's briefly refer back to the Patterning and Beliefs section to recap:

- I was born and raised on a council estate – so there was never enough.

- I was the poorest of my friends at school – I always felt like the outcast who didn't belong—hanging out in their mansions.

- I had Daddy issues – always trying to impress my father and never felt good enough.

- In young adulthood, I was abused by men and felt vulnerable – I was angry and wanted to assert my power and, again, prove my worth.

Combined, these four sets of circumstances, and their associated challenges, have created a bit of a monster.

This beast can, if left unchecked, drive me to insanity as I compete against my own inner critics – I become a workaholic, striveaholic, never-quite-cutting-the-mustardaholic.

I've ventured down that dark 'obsessive nutcase' tunnel many a time—teetering on the brink of collapse from pressure, dissatisfaction, perfectionism and yet more striving.

But then, I saw the light – and so can you.

First, do the inner work from the previous module. Then, you can connect with your REAL reason to exist in this world.

The Big Why

Sod worthlessness, why bother with that negative energy, when you can realise your value and connect with your true purpose. Your gift. Your soul's intended path.

Although they both make you move your ass, your 'Big Why' is very different to 'The Strive'. Striving is a different beast altogether, it's very needy, greedy and 'getty'.

Whereas your 'Big Why' energy is a great ball of abundant love. It is the passion that ignites your every cell and lifts you up. The thing that makes you jump up and shout *'HELL YEAH!'* —You are so destined to fulfil this mission.

You have a very unique gift. You *are* a very unique gift. You have a message to deliver to the world, and there's only you qualified to do so. It's your reason for being.

If you took away every inhibition and limitation, what would you want to do? If you removed your self-consciousness, and brazenly declared your talent—what would it be?

What fuels the fire in your belly?

False Fuel vs. True Fire

What motivates you? Are you money motivated? Or are you joy motivated?

Think about that one for a minute.

Why are you motivated by money? What will it bring you?

A Ferrari?

And why do you want a Ferrari?

Is it because it'll make you look cool on social media? Do you think that will make you happy? Popular? Attractive?

Is it really money that is motivating you? Or is it the end result?

The momentary joy between getting the keys and realising said supercar isn't ticking your deep-rooted boxes, is short-lived. So what happens when your fancy wheels don't actually fix your life?

Hmmmm… Buyers remorse!

How about skipping the Ferrari, and all the squillions of quids needed to purchase said shiny red diva, and just going straight for joy?

This is what happens when you align with your Big Why.

Striving you see, is constant. *There's no arriving, whilst ever you're striving!*

You never quite make it to the field of contentment.

The Big Why, on the other hand, delivers fulfilment from the moment you decide that's where you are heading. Just saying it, immediately releases peace of mind into your veins—calming the cortisol from your previous striving ways. And that feeling is a gift you'll never want to return to the showroom!

I am living proof of this right now.

For donkey's years I have suppressed my desire to write. I imagined that if I could build a business, create a passive income, and buy my freedom, I could then travel and write to my heart's content.

So off I set, multiple times over, on various business adventures – none of which were my one true purpose.

My purpose is to write, to teach. *And to party and flounce, of course!*

ALL of these businesses were set up to make money.

Don't get me wrong, we've had successes and fun along the way. And they have all formed a distinct part of the path — the necessary bends in the road.

But nevertheless, that moment, in the hospital when I made my heartfelt declaration to God and started writing this book—I connected with my joy.

And that joy has stood by me and lit me up—even though I've been dealing with the biggest challenges of business to date.

The fact that I'm living my purpose has given me the strength to lean into the chaos and actually enjoy the feeling of being alive. Every awkward conversation and painful encounter has been something to be grateful for – a new message to deliver to the world, wrapped up here for you, in my first literary gift.

For me, the pain now has a joy connection. I am learning how to feel sublime whilst absolute mayhem plays out in the background.

Not only am I journalling as I go, but I am uncovering truths, solutions and stories to share with you. So that I can bring you up with me. I am scribing the chaos away—and I feel freer, and more joyful, than I have in years.

I am comforted by my faith and trust in the universe. Tenderly guided by my own guru and motivated by passion—the true source of abundance. I'm happier than I've ever been. Just living my truth. And that truth is there, inside of you too.

Sometimes, a massive leap of faith is in order to reach it. Other times, chaos and collapse walk in with a Universal warrant for destruction, leaving you with no choice but to face your truth.

In any case, you have an opportunity now, to dig deep, have a chat with your intuition, your guru of all gurus, and pull out your purpose. What will you find?

Exercise

Take the opportunity and ask yourself the following questions.

- What do I actually want to do with my time?

- Where in my life am I striving to prove something?

- What do I feel truly passionate about?

- What do I want to be remembered for?

- 'What message is mine alone to deliver?

Light a candle, sit with these questions, write without filtering – take a leaf out of my book (literally) and pour your soul out onto the pages. Get this right, and the switch from toxic striving energy to high-vibing peace and joy, is instantaneous.

Now that your 'Big Why' is lit, we're ready to start generating the sparks. Prepare to switch your lights fully on.

14

Sparks

Bright ideas from one's wildest imagination

Hey Bright Spark! You ready for some fun?

We're now in the void of pure potentiality—that magical space where the storm has been and gone, washing away all the nonk that you never needed anyway.

Now you have a blank canvas. A set of paints. And your beautifully creative mind.

But first, before you can craft your colour-infused dream life, you need a clear vision.

And the best visions are ignited with a spark.

A spark of inspiration. Of genius. An idea, a download—call it what you like.

Your spark will light your soul fire, fuelling the passion that propels you forward – the true motivating factor.

So, how do you get a spark?

'Come with me, and you'll see, there's a world of pure imagination.'[26] Remember the iconic line from *Willy Wonka and the Chocolate Factory?*[26]

As kids, we had 3 pre-recorded VCRs. My mum had acquired them—perfectly legitimately, I'm sure (ahem), from a dodgy bloke down at the working men's club.

Anyhow, we had *Willy Wonka,*[26] *Mary Poppins,*[27] and *The Never-Ending Story*[6]—a magnificent selection of wondrous films. No surprise, then, that I have the imagination of a neuromagical unicorn—on acid. I watched these three deliciously bonkers delights on repeat throughout my individuation years.

But *Willy Wonka and the Chocolate Factory*[26] – oh my, that was my favourite—that opening scene! Oodles and boodles of chocolate being seductively poured into trays—how I longed to be one of those trays!

Oh, I would have been so stuck up that chute with Augustus Gloop!

And that line in the song sums it all up for me. *'Come with me, and you'll see, there's a world of pure imagination.'*[26]

As far as I'm concerned, the world *is* made from pure imagination! Every *thing* that exists, was once a spark of imagination.

Imagination is so incredibly powerful, especially when combined with intuition. These JV partners can change the world.

Every epiphany throughout history has come to realisation during a moment of mindfulness – when imagination and intuition have been given the stage for a few moments.

Isaac Newton realised gravity when sitting beneath a tree, Archimedes named displacement, his 'Eureka!' moment, whilst soaking in the bath.

Countless other life-changing sparks have arrived during peaceful moments of solace.

So, we need a technique to crack you open and release your inner artist.

It's time to adventure deep inside, to discover your wildest dreams!

Let's crack you open.

So where do they come from? These epiphany clouds that float into our minds' ears from time to time? Whispering their tempting little tales of excitement.

They come from the void. Remember—that thing left over, after a good onslaught of chaos?

The void—a warehouse with every item you could possibly desire. It's just invisible until you believe it. In other words, it's a space holder for *ANYTHING* you can dream of.

But before you can place your order, you need to allow the void into your life. Which is *not* always easy.

As humans, in this day and age, our nervous systems are bombarded 24/7. What with all the noise and disruption of daily life. Being beholden to everybody else's dramas at any second—thanks to social media. We're literally on call 24 hours a day to anybody who has our number. I mean, 'on call' used to mean 'at work'. Nowadays, 'on call' means 'alive'—as we have our phones strapped to us at all times.

So...

You need to connect fully with your superpowers, to allow the sparks to fall in. That means allowing yourself some peace. This is going to involve ditching that block of nuisance (yes, your phone) from time to time, even just for an hour to take a phoneless walk, to finally let your mind think for itself again.

If you can brave a half day without touching that sleek, techy temptress, you'll be floored by the revelations that start pouring in

In the good old days (pre-2010), people would debate internally—we would even have full-blown arguments with ourselves to work things out. This is so important.

The great leaders and philosophers of this world all have something in common: they all set aside time to think. Time to just be, with their own thoughts, and then to be without them.

Nowadays, we don't even try to think. We just Google it. And that's fine if it's an instant fact you're seeking. But t'interweb hasn't got your unique soul-led intuitive thoughts in there!

When was the last time you were alone with your thoughts for half an hour?

Some do actually just call it 'thinking time', others call it meditation. I've also heard 'focus hour'. Others go for a run, or a walk, *sans* phone. They appreciate the value of letting their minds roam free.

In all cases, no matter how they format this time, the most successful humans on Earth (and in space) prioritise quiet time, away from the noise and the nonsense.

They don't lose a whole day on TikTok. Successful people use social media to sell their businesses. In stark contrast, the majority of the population are used by social media—the 'sold to'.

'She lived a long life, but mostly on Instagram'—imagine if that was your epitaph!

The ultra successful use their phones as business tools. Not as crutches. They appreciate the value of time spent inside their own heads.

They think, they daydream, they meditate, they transcend.

This was reaffirmed, like magic, literally days after I first drafted this chapter.

One of my mentors posted her morning routine on LinkedIn. From waking at 5:30am until starting work at 9:30am, it consists of mind-clearing, soul-steadying processes such as meditation, journalling and planning. All of this is prioritised, by a woman who successfully runs multiple multi-million-pound businesses, whilst maintaining an ever-calm and professional demeanour. It's no surprise that she never mentioned scrolling Facebook over a bowl of Cocoa Pops, is it?!

So, I'm going to ask you to do something a little bit terrifying now. I'm going to ask you to commit to at least an hour a day of phone-free 'me time' for the next 28 days.

And no, when you're asleep doesn't count! This must be during your usually active and present hours.

If you can do this, allow yourself this indulgence into your inner world, I can bet you a Wonka bar that you will adore this new enlightened state.

I would recommend a half hour of reflection/meditation at the beginning of the day, and again at the end. But if you can squeeze in a midday or afternoon mindful walk or meditation, that is going to be transformational as it breaks up the noise of the day.

I'm not going to tell you what your focus method should be. It could be a solo activity such as walking or cycling. It could be a deep transcendental meditation. The type of activity is not important, it's the clarity of mind that is.

In this state, your senses, including your sixth sense, will reignite – and those sparks will flow in!

I can just imagine my teenager's face if I dared impress this suggestion upon her. The younger you are, the more terrifying the thought of this task—but, of course, the greater the results.

I was barely still a teen when mobile phones hit the mainstream, so I had time to develop my imagination, pre-'box-attached-to-face' pandemic.

But for those of you who carried your mobile in through the birth canal, you might not have ever really had the opportunity yet to explore your consciousness. Prepare to blow your mind!

But most of us—a little longer in the tooth, have simply forgotten how to 'be'. How can you 'just be' with a constant nattering and buzzing going off all the time? It's relentless.

Think of all the people who are 'in' your phone – either contacts or social media followers. Now imagine that they all just appeared in your bedroom as you're just getting comfortable for the night.

Would you still feel comfortable?

Would you *buggery*! You'd feel violated, self-conscious, disturbed, overwhelmed, confused, crowded, everything that is *really uncomfortable*.

So why is it that you take your phone to bed with you every night? And why is it the first thing you look at in the morning? Isn't that a bit creepy?

Also, do you know, those few minutes, when you first wake, and also when you are settled and ready for sleep, are your most intuitively connected and most subconsciously impressionable moments.

So, if you're wasting this opportunity for brilliance and healing, and trading it for toxicating tales of everybody else's lives, dramas, trials and tribulations, then you're doing yourself a huge disservice.

Have you ever lain awake all night because you are enraged about the unkind opinions of an easily offended keyboard-warrior? And even when you do nod off – your dreams and subconscious tuning are aligned with that drama, and not your chosen path of peace, freedom and love.

Maybe, it's time to rebel and say no to the thing that everybody else does. To make the choice to stop the noise.

So go on—ditch the noise, make space for sparks, and see what magic floats in.

I meditate twice daily as a matter of course.

I may have decided to hang up my property developer boots for the foreseeable, but for the seven years that I was in the thick of it, I used meditation – onsite, often covered in dust and muck, to download my design inspirations.

The team used to think (still do, in fact) that I'm a bit of a batty bird! I'd sit cross-legged, in the middle of a dusty room, piles of rubble everywhere, channelling the energy of the house.

When creating the design plan for The Burgoyne Hotel, I connected via meditation with the history, until each perfect spark had fallen into place.

Your mind is an open portal to a universe of infinite sparks, if you'd only leave that door open to allow them in!

Of course, not all ideas are worth actioning, some may be VERY random! You do need to be choosy actually, as it's not practical to roll with them all. But once you open up that creative flow, you can learn to focus the technique so that the ideas become relevant to your chosen niche, strategy or path.

Your genius is inside. Just waiting its turn to speak up.

So, to summarise, ditch the phone, practice solitude for at least an hour a day, and focus only on the sparks which are relevant to your cause.

Exercise

Now then my love, go grab your journal and write down the answers to the following questions:

- Where were you when you received a life-changing idea?

- What distractions might be blocking your sparks?

- What are the top five sparks you never acted on?

Ready for greatness? Come with me my lovely, into the next chapter—This shizzle is about to get real!

15

Hocus Focus Pocus

Congratulations, you have the sparks of greatness —
Now it's time to Hocus Focus Pocus them into reality!

Hocus Pocus[28] may be the best Halloween film of all time (in my opinion, darlings). But it's also a super magical phrase—the very words uttered by any self-respecting witch as she commands her latest spell to take form.

But is it really magic? Or just a dramatisation of something that's been happening since time began?

Manifestation

A lot of us have tried intentional manifestation. Probably years ago, when we read *The Secret*[29]—and the next day we infamously manifested a parking spot, exactly where we intended it to be! Shocker!

The thing is though, most of us do this *only* once. Then we put it down to chance—we fail to recognise ourselves as great creators—because our naughty little egos pop up and tell us not to be so daft.

We talk ourselves out of the 'plain sight truth' – because it's easier to accept our mediocrity if we had no hand in creating it. *Wowzers!* Now there's a sucker punch your Truth Fairy would be proud of!

It's back to our programming, you see.

We are misinformed as children to believe that we are weak, vulnerable and in danger of the world happening to us at any moment. No wonder our minds are blown at the thought of a cosmic car park manipulation!

On the other side of the coin, the most successful people in the world *do* believe in manifestation. They didn't get the heebie-jeebies the first time it worked. So they went on to sculpt their lives and create their heart-felt desires—the living proof.

So, is manifestation real? Or a completely fantastical concept?

Are sorcery and conjurement for an exclusive few? The fiendish immortals, who rarely have the best intentions?

Or could it be, that this mysterious process of commanding one's wildest dreams from the ether, is actually available to all? *Sans* full moon and dragons' blood?

Because maybe, that one time, when you had a go and blew your own socks off with your car park dominatrix powers, it was real!

And buggering hell, perhaps the reason that it never worked since, is because your mind was full of doubt?

You'd have had to have been living under a rock for the past few years if you haven't heard of manifestation. It's a serious source of controversy – mainly because those who use it to their advantage, believe in it. And those who don't, well, don't.

So, let's have a look at the manifestation debate. Word of mouth is the best recommendation, right? Let's see who has said what about the Universal Law of Attraction.

The OGs

Jesus Christ

"Ask, and it shall be given you; seek, and ye shall find; knock, and the door shall be opened unto you."[30]
– (Matthew 7:7 – the ultimate OG manifestation instruction.)

Earl Nightingale

"We become what we think about."[31]

– From *The Strangest Secret*, the 1956 recording that kicked off the modern personal development movement.

Andrew Carnegie

"Any idea that is held in the mind, that is emphasised, that is either feared or revered, will begin at once to clothe itself in the most convenient and appropriate physical forms available."[32]

– A hidden gem of Carnegie's legacy, echoing the law of attraction long before the phrase was coined.

Louise Hay

"I do not fix problems. I fix my thinking. Then problems fix themselves."[33]

– From *You Can Heal Your Life*, showing how internal shifts ripple out into external reality.

Dr Wayne Dyer

"You'll see it when you believe it."[34]

– A beautiful reversal of the 'seeing is believing' conditioning demonstrated in the 'Hallucinations' chapter.

Deepak Chopra

"The universe has no fixed agenda. Once you make any decision, it works around that decision. There is no right or wrong – only a series of possibilities that shift with each thought, feeling, and action that you experience."[35]

– From *The Spontaneous Fulfilment of Desire*,[35] which literally blends quantum science with mystical truth.

Modern Manifestors

Oprah Winfrey

"You don't become what you want. You become what you believe."[36]

– Oprah's entire life is a testament to the power of intention. She openly attributes her success to mastering mindset and alignment.

Jim Carrey

"I wrote myself a cheque for ten million dollars for "acting services rendered" and dated it Thanksgiving 1995. I kept it in my wallet, and just before Thanksgiving 1995, I got paid ten million dollars for Dumb and Dumber."[37]

– One of the most legendary stories of visualisation and belief in action.

Lady Gaga

*"I used to walk down the street like I was a f*ing star… I just knew it was going to happen. I saw it."*[38]

– She credits *embodied belief* as the driving force behind her rise, years before fame came.

Just look at this epic list – this is literally a teeny, tiny, cocktail-sausage-sized snippet of the esteemed following that manifestation has. It just cannot be denied.

So What About the Sceptics?

'Manifesting? Mindset? What a load of woo-woo!' the cynical crowd scoff.

Only because they haven't mastered it—and being a non-master of anything doesn't feel good. So, the obvious human thing to do is to reject it. But don't get drawn into scepticism.

Just as you wouldn't ask an egg for advice on how to be a sausage—the same goes for manifesting. They just don't know what they don't know.

So, are there people out there who are wildly successful and joyfully aligned—without *any* belief in mindset or manifestation?

In short: *no.*

You might encounter the occasional multi-millionaire who rolls their eyes at 'energy work' or 'spiritual alignment.' But look closer, and what you'll notice is that they're still *doing it.* They may not call it magic, but they still wield it.

You see, when you set a clear intention, believe in your own power, hold an unwavering emotional vision, and take aligned action, you're manifesting—whether you call it that or not.

So, next time someone tries to tell you that manifestation isn't real, just smile. You don't need to argue. Just know, in that knowing way, that they're doing it.

How does it work? This manifestation malarkey?

Here are the practical steps:

- **Hocus** – Have the thought. What is it that you would like to manifest?

- **Focus** – Hold your focus on that thought, enhance this by aligning your physiological state. This can be done under meditation; chanting sets you on the right frequency for attracting. Go deep and feel the emotional connection to that which you want to bring into reality. To become a true power manifestor you must not miss the 'Focus' from your 'Hocus Pocus'. Focus is the key to success.

- **Pocus** – And it shall manifest. Perhaps not in a puff of smoke, and sometimes not in the form you expect, or in the requested timeframe. But it shall arrive, when the universe decrees that the time is right. Just know that it is done.

It may sound like witchcraft, but it's entirely doable.

You already manifest everything within your life on a daily basis. Wouldn't you like to have some directorship over that?

Manifestation, in fact, creation, is something that is going to happen whether you try to control it or not. 'Stuff' is going to appear in your virtual reality every day. And – guess what my love, that stuff is out of control until you take control.

It's like water. Channelled and controlled, it becomes a beautiful canal, not just pretty and calming, but a means to deliver supplies where they are needed. Water, when focused and distributed intelligently, is the lifeblood of the planet.

But, out of control, water is a tsunami, a flood – a deluge.

In both cases, water is the same substance. The difference behind it is *intention*.

Thoughts, just like water, with set intention and focus, can create a masterful framework of success in your life.

But thoughts that come in like a monsoon, unexpected, and all-consuming, have the power to drown you.

So please, take the time each day to create the channels—so your thoughts and intentions flow in the right direction.

The Manifestation of Moolah

Now, let me tell you about one of my manifestations.

Back in early 2021, the house we'd been buying for months — Hillthorpe Manor — almost slipped through our fingers. The mortgage was in place, and the deposit was sitting in the bank. Then, without warning, and just a week prior to completion, the bank decided that due to Covid, they would no longer accept dividends as income. The mortgage offer was pulled.

The vendor gave us one week to sort it, or she'd sell it to the next highest bidder. It was our dream home: my daughters even had a horse living in the stables next door. We were fully invested in this move. I sobbed as I felt the dream dissolving. But then, something shifted.

I said 'No.'

I went deep into meditation — and Om-ed the fear out of my system. I realised I'd been acting like I believed the house was ours, but deep down, I'd never actually *felt* it. So, in my trance state, I fell in love with Hillthorpe. I connected with her energy. I gave her a personality and created a spiritual bond. I told her we were in this together.

Then I opened my laptop, focused intently and took the actions that came to me during the meditation. Within 72 hours, I'd raised £400,000. We exchanged contracts on the Monday. And the rest is Hillthorpe history.

Manifestation isn't just chanting and vision boards (although I did pull out the stops and include these too!) It's deep alignment, *combined* with radical action.

There's a famous Quaker saying – when you pray, move your feet.[39] It's so true. Controlling your thoughts puts you in charge of your emotions, and when you combine that with the right action – your desired result cannot help but show up.

Your thoughts become things – this is the truest thing you might ever disbelieve.

It's so weird that we object to our 'powers' so much. We are convinced that manifestation isn't a thing, yet we do it constantly. Sometimes, not exactly on purpose.

Do you really want that?

You drive past McDonald's, and the image of a McPlant meal invades your thoughts. You focus on it. Then comes a tummy rumble. Next thing, you're in the drive through. The thought is now in your hand – manifested in burger form!

The physiological response (hunger pang) led to the action (swerving violently into the drive through) to get a fast-food fix that you didn't even know you wanted (because you didn't) until you saw that big yellow M.

McDonald's are fully aware that if they infiltrate your thoughts – you are likely to take it through the full manifestation process!

So, are you going to allow yourself to conjure willy-nilly results forever? Or are you going to admit that it's a thing, learn to control what you think and practice focus?

Damnit, I'm only writing this analogy as a demonstration for you, and now I want a flipping McPlant! This stuff works!

It's so obvious when the penny drops.

And this magic is available to *everybody*. You don't need to be born into wealth. You just need to be *willing*—to believe, to act, and to wait.

Now, if there's one more thing I need you to take from this chapter, it's this: *manifestation only works when you do.*

Because here's my confession:

I stopped.

For about a year, I didn't do my meditations at all. Life got busy. I was focused on fixing things. Surviving. But in that space, while I stopped connecting with my higher self, *the worst happened.*

The fraud. The fallout. And the near-collapse of my business.

I was spiralling. It wasn't just external chaos—I was energetically vulnerable too. I had disconnected from the frequency of creation. And what happens when you're not in charge of your frequency? You attract chaos.

When I started writing this book, it reminded me, I hadn't been living it quite as much as I preach. So, I restarted my practice. Morning meditations. Evening visualisations. Every day. Without fail. And what's happened since has been nothing short of miraculous.

Angels have shown up all over the place – opportunities far grander than I could ever have dreamed of. I've found my peace. I'm living my joy. All since going all in on the one thing that controls this reality – myself.

That's the real magic of manifestation.

But you won't see any of it if you're stuck in survival mode.

If you're fogged up with doubt and fear.

If you're not vibrating at the frequency where these opportunities can *reach you.*

So please, *don't stop the practice.*

As a natural born rebel, I fricking hate routines. But this is one discipline I now abide by, no matter what.

190

Don't ignore the power of your mind.

Hocus. Focus. Pocus.

Take your spark and manifest it into reality.

The tragedy is that so many people see the spark but don't act on it. They doubt. They wait. They think the idea was silly, unrealistic, or 'not for someone like me.'

But you're not someone like them: *you're reading this.*

Everyday Manifestation – Your Basic Spell-work

Let's get really clear now. It's one thing to understand manifestation—but another thing entirely to practise it daily with power and intent.

So here are some no-nonsense, high-frequency principles to anchor your intention:

- **Your words are wands.**
  Everything you speak is a declaration of your intentions to the Universe. Speak with intention. Speak with care. Be really careful what you wish for.

- **Negative thoughts are squatters – don't let them move in.**
  You *will* have them. That's human. But do not entertain them. Do not feed them. Notice them, bless them, and show them the door. Let them pass like

clouds. And remember that the sunshine always comes back out. Because every thought you entertain plants a seed—and you don't want to grow weeds!

- **Bless what you already have.**
  Take some money in your hand and bless it. Thank it. Feel the richness of even the smallest amount. Gratitude turns pennies into pounds.

- **Become conscious of the free-flowing abundance around you.**
  Everything is energy. You're already living in the substance you want more of. The question is—are you noticing it? Are you celebrating it? Awareness is the switch that turns the lights on.

In case you've forgotten—here's your final reminder. If manifestation were a spell, it would look something like this: *Hocus (Thought)* → *Focus (Emotion/Frequency)* → *Pocus (Trust/Surrender)*.

If you honour the practice, remember the Spark, feel the feeling, and show up with your greatest intentions, then what you seek will not only find you,

It will *run* to you. Like Kevin Costner in *The Bodyguard*.[40]

Because what you can see in your mind and feel in your body—you can hold in your hand.

That is true creation. And you, my love, were born for it.

Now, go manifest something breathtaking. You absolute freaking wizard!

By the way, wizard energy is in the next chapter, so stay on this high frequency and come with me for a masterclass – become the all-powerful joy-magnet that you are!

16

Energy and Vibration

Carefree wild abandon, love, peace and joy are my natural energy states—my gifts to share with fellow adventurers on this kaleidoscopic rollercoaster called life!

If there's one word that sums up the catalyst behind manifestation, it's energy.

Energy is the force that sits behind everything. You are energy. I am energy. The universe is a mish mash of energies, all buzzing with creative prowess and limitless potentiality.

Energy can be set to various frequencies or *vibrations*.

It's all good having your 'spark' and knowing the 'Hocus Focus Pocus' technique. But if some keyboard warrior has just given you a dressing down on Facebook, for declaring that you put the jam on your scone before the cream (*attack of the whingers!*), then you might not be energetically fit for focused manifestation. You need to clear those chakras first, my love!

Do you believe in vibrations?

Have you ever walked into a room and, before anybody has said anything, you felt like you could 'cut the atmosphere with a knife?'

And on the flip side, have you ever met somebody for the first time, who immediately makes you smile and want to be silly?

This energy is set by the frequency of the vibrations in your presence at the time. And the frequency directly controls the goods that come to you that day.

One cannot vibrate on the level of a fart, my dear, and expect to attract roses!

If you can master the control of your energetic state, you have mastered your life.

But this is no mean feat. Because we are all so affected by our jabbering monkey minds, as well as other peoples' energy, and other folks' dramas, too.

I'd like to hark back to the *Peanuts* chapter here, and remind you of the energy vampires who literally sap the colour out of your cheeks.

They should be avoided. I also steer clear of the news. It's always bad news, isn't it? Some folks are offended by the fact that I don't watch it. As if I'm shirking my responsibility to have to feel the death and destruction. But, considering that I am a change-maker, I don't think that me being in an eternal state of sorrow is going to help me make positive waves. I'd rather live in a bubble of ignorant bliss, and create from this space, than be deflated by a one-sided doom show.

Over-sensitivity too, can cause a drop in energy. Are you easily offended? There are so many things to be offended about. Words mean different things to different people. They are just vehicles to describe how we feel. And people don't interpret that in the same way as one another.

For example, I call everybody 'love' – in Yorkshire, it's a thing. Some women find it offensive to be called 'love', especially by a man. But if that man is a Yorkshireman, he says it as a greeting, not a chat up line! He calls his best mate Derek down at the pub, 'love', too. He's not trying to get into Derek's pants!

In Newcastle, you get called 'pet' – it doesn't mean they're calling you a dog. Or a rat. But even if they did, why is an animal seen as an offensive thing?

I find all of these terms very endearing. But some don't.

Do you see what I mean? It's the *intention* behind the word that is offensive rather than the word itself, so think about whether it was said with kindness or with venom, then give people some slack and preserve your own joy by keeping your righteousness in check. You don't want to be the energy vampire!

— The Truth Fairy

The biggest energy sapper of all is a little something called 'worry'.

I'll tell you why - because you are never worrying about the present moment. Yet you are tainting the now— the only moment that you ever have in life, with a feeling of guilt or dread from something that has been and gone. Or you're investing an inordinate amount of energy into an imaginary future scenario—that may not happen.

I get it, it's hard not to worry. But it doesn't help. And you can decide not to. I do it all the time, people are always asking me 'how do you sleep at night?' and saying things like 'I don't know how you cope with all the stress'.

I do sleep, and I do cope, because most of the time I choose not to worry. It doesn't serve and in fact often makes the problem worse as you can't make an informed decision from a place of worry.

Do you know anybody who is a 'worrier'?

Of course, everybody does, right! Does that person have a confident, can-do attitude? Are they a yes person who lives life to the full? Are they highly successful in a 'contented glowing from within' kind of way?

Point taken!

The worrier is a seeker of doom and is often consumed with another great life-sapper—'*LACK*'. Oh Jeez! Not lack! Not worry of lack! How catastrophic life is when we worry tremendously about an imaginary event that could potentially cause us to lose something that doesn't really matter that much.

What if I run out of money? What if the utility bills rise and I can't eat? What if I lose my job? What if I don't get my bonus this year? What if interest rates go up?

What if, what if, what if…

Shut up, you boring, bloody doom merchant! When has any of that actually caused you to starve?

Like, never!

Worry gets passed around from person to person like an evil spliff, intoxicating their heads with impending doom!

What if, what if, from the evil spliff!

But…

What if all of your dreams come true? What if lack is never a thing? What if the universe always actually delivers exactly what you need, when you need it? *Hmmm?* Isn't that what has always happened?

It's time for you to identify these traits in yourself. None of us are immune to worry, lack, over-sensitivity and other people's dramas. Have a good honest chat with yourself and lift the veil on your own energy swipers.

Realise this one thing. All of these energetic hindrances hail from putting importance on that which is not really important. This is the number one cause of your own suffering. See that, and you're winning again. Awareness is everything!

But, cutting these toxicity magnets out of your life doesn't necessarily mean you're going to side-step negativity altogether… For this, you need to become a Frequency Ninja!

The real power lies in internal mastery.

Frequency Ninjas are unaffected by these glum companions and remain in their higher states of consciousness despite the mayhem. Because they have honed their vibratory skills to ensure only the highest heights are maintained.

What are you vibing on right now? Think about it.

The Frequency Ninja has the ability to bypass the lower states, and they know that:

Frequency resonates with frequency,

Opposite frequencies repel each other - like magnets.

You are susceptible to picking up the energy of others.

The thing is, as we can't see them, or hear them, most people have no concept of their frequency.

It's funny really as we all believe in microwaves and radio – and just like a ready-made meal, we see and live the results of our frequencies every day. But, for some reason, we can't compute or believe in our own frequencies.

So, to counteract our doubts, let's visualise: imagine frequencies are like infinite washing lines going through space.

On the wealth line, you'll find a shit tonne of money, diamonds, yachts—Richard Branson, for goodness' sake! Smiling and waving from his hot air balloon of fulfilment!

And guess what? You can only access these things *IF* you're also pegged up on the wealth line.

As soon as you have a doubt, worry about money, or are stricken by Imposter Syndrome—you are going to drop like a lead weight towards the poverty line — here you'll find bills, angry faces, and suffering. All the nasty Norris's!

You can, however, get out of that low frequency by snuggling a playful puppy for instance. A puppy knows nothing but unconditional love and joy - puppy vibes! So, snuggle that puppy and you'll soon be back on the love line—the highest of them all.

The puppy — faithful companion of every Frequency Ninja!

What does this fanciful, laundry-inspired tale tell you?

That's right, we're all impressionable little sausages who, in one fell swoop, can be knocked off the high vibe, and onto the lower levels - *if* we allow ourselves to be affected.

What to Do When the Frequency Drops

Furry friends and joking aside, when we are on that higher frequency, and aligned with all the good stuff, we really want to stay there. Up there we are a magnet for great things, and the bad shit, well we may be able to see it – but we don't need to get involved in it.

Let the neg heads float by, and don't allow them to draw you in. Stay tuned in to the frequency of abundance. Do not lower yourself to the plane of debt, distress and victimhood. *Nothing can come into your existence - unless you summon it with persistent thoughts,* so just don't. Keep yourself pegged up in the right place.

You are completely in charge of your energy!

Tip for 'meh' Days

Sometimes, we all have a day where we are just sad for no apparent reason. It might be hormonal. Other times, there's no rhyme or reason. My best advice for days like this is to just let them be. Don't spend hours driving yourself into a worse state of anxiety because you are worried about why you feel depressed – over analysis will just drive you into a spiral.

And don't try to create on days like this either.

This is not the day to raise finance.

Definitely don't have that 'awkward conversation' with an employee.

Or bring up the fact that your husband left his undercrackers on the floor - again.

Any of these actions, coming from a place of doom, will undoubtedly end in carnage.

This is a day to ignore the world and concentrate on one thing and one thing only – *feeling better*. Stay in bed and sleep it off—*hibernate*. Treat yourself to a soak in the bath.

Meditate *all day*. Stuff your face with chocolate – yes chocolate, *f**k survival of the fittest, sometimes it's survival of the fattest* and we just need to get through the day!

So, indulge yourself on this day.

Create only when you feel better. Because you don't want to manifest a turd! Unless you are constipated, of course!

Picture these feelings as heavy, dark clouds. Let them consume you for a moment. Feel into the sadness. Appreciate it for what it is – a demonstration of life. Let those clouds rain tears all over you, and have a deep heartfelt sob to release that energy.

The cloud will soon disperse, they always do—the sun always comes back out.

Know this, and just accept that sadness, in small doses, is ok.

Sadness, self-pity, fear and other negative states can be reversed, however. *(It's ok to hang out there for a day or two, but sadness is not for long-term rental my love).*

When you adopt a frequency that doesn't serve you, simply uplift again by practicing the Frequency Ninja Power Moves below.

Power Move 1: Chanting

Chanting meditations create a strong vibration throughout your whole body. These vibrations alter your physiology to match the frequency of the chant – and each chant has a purpose.

My two favourite chants—the ones that I practice daily, are the chants of *ah,*[41] and *om,*[41]. *Ah*[41] is the manifestation frequency. *Om*[41] is the frequency that allows you to surrender all to the universe.

They are the tools that I use to raise my vibration at any moment. I do *ah*[41] on a morning, and *om*[41] every evening. In the chanting state, you become a conductor of pure universal energy, bringing it into your being. You are literally plugging yourself in to the limitless universal flow.

Even if you think this is an absolute load of nonk, I urge you to have a go. It only takes 20 minutes, and you will feel amazing afterwards. The physical effect of chanting, therefore creating these sound vibrations throughout your own body, is nothing short of miraculous itself. You will feel like a buzzy powerpack of bliss afterwards – bursting with energetic potential.

Power Move 2: Gratitude

Another tool for raising your frequency instantly is gratitude.

Being thankful for everything in your life now – for life itself, for your family, for your health, the sunshine, for the car that you're driving around in—all of it. We have so much to be grateful for, no matter what mayhem is going on around us.

When we're on that poverty line, we can fall into victim mentality and create a 'poor me' story. Don't get caught up in *only-ness*: I only have this, and I am only that.

Mental Anguish = Physical Anguish.

You can untie those stomach knots instantly, raise your abundance thermostat, and release all negativity with a calming and reassuring dose of gratitude.

Make your declarations out loud. Describe in detail every little thing that you can be thankful for in that moment. Each intention of thanksgiving will erase one of the energetic knots that's holding you back.

My friend, Sefton,[42] yoga and breathwork guru, steps outside every morning, opens his arms out wide, and says thank you to the sky. What a beautiful way to start the day, saying thank you to the huge expanse of love and support of the universe. Go do that now, every morning.

Sefton would be thrilled to know that you, as I, have adopted this discipline. It's the simplest thing, it takes seconds. But it creates a massive shift in your consciousness.

Exercise: The Control Centre

Close your eyes and picture your control centre inside your mind. Visualise the panel of switches in front of you. See them all laid out, little golden flicker switches, each labelled:

- Awaken
- Joy
- Love
- Confidence
- Flow
- Foresight
- Charisma
- Self-belief
- Success
- Abundance
- Relaxation

Flick them all on. Hear the clicks, and see the light emit brightly from inside your soul as each one is activated.

They are always there. You decide when to bring them into play.

You wouldn't attempt to fly a plane without turning all of the systems on, would you?

It's the same with your switches: turn them all on and watch how you rise, how you soar, how your energy inflates—how you flow your way to success, time after time, even if you're not a particularly elegant bird!

"I wouldn't board your plane if you weren't prepared to activate the necessary systems for flight – so why would you?"
– The Truth Fairy

Energy is the key to success. And flicking it on – every day, is the fast track to energetic alignment.

Practicing these energy boosting disciplines on a daily basis will give you Universal Credits – no, not the ones you sign on at the Job Centre for, but the great blessings and rewards of abundance that the universe has lined up for you.

There are no limits. Energy flows where focus goes.

In no time at all, you will earn your Frequency Ninja Badge and you'll be rising up all over the shop. You are now in a state to Hocus, Focus flipping Pocus your socks off and create the life of your dreams.

How much are you buzzing right now?

You have the mastery tools in your box. And now it's time to actualise these methods by combining them with a plan—to create your new reality.

So, bring your wildest dreams into the next module, as we orchestrate your purposeful life.

Right here, right now, is when the theory stops, and the reality begins.

Don your Frequency Ninja mask, and take my hand - let's get this flow on the road!

Module 4

Orchestration

Right, darling. Enough collapsing, confessing, and cosmic sparking. You've survived the worst, stared into the mirror of honesty, and lit the sparks of awakening—now it's time to get your shit together.

This is where the dream becomes a design, the chaos becomes a chorus, and you finally start conducting life instead of being dragged behind it like a tin can on a wedding car.

Now, my love, it's time to orchestrate.

This is the turning point—you're knocking on the door of success now—in that truly magical space in the arc where chaos dissolves completely and shapes itself into something intentional.

Here, your scattered ideas, visions, and truths stop blowing around like confetti in a storm and begin to gather into harmony.

In these chapters, you'll learn how to spot and follow the path of least resistance, so you're no longer flogging dead horses, but flowing where life opens up.

You'll anchor yourself with the Rebellion Life Philosophy, a compass that keeps you true when the world gets noisy.

You'll craft your vision of Heaven on Earth, dream bigger than you ever dared, and then explore how to create purposeful income—money that feels as good to make as it feels to spend.

You'll step boldly into the spotlight and bring yourself fully to the party, no masks, no shrinking, just the unapologetic YOU Show.

Finally, you'll pull it all together with The Plan—your rebel roadmap, the document that turns dreams into action and makes bloody magic happen.

This is where you stop surviving chaos and start conducting it. This is where life stops playing you—and you become the maestro of your own symphony.

Wow! What a module! You ready to raise the baton with me?

17

The Path of Least Resistance

The universe will let you know when you're scrambling up the wrong hill – by blasting you off sideways.

How many roads must a man walk down? Before you can call him a man?[43] Well, I don't know about being called a man, Bob Dylan, but try walking down too many paths, and you'll be fricking exhausted!

There are so many routes to success out there – too many. But they are *not* all for you.

It's easy to get swept along though, with the hype and the fads. Because everybody who *is* on their correct path, will want you to join them.

Don't.

Learn from them, yes. But take your own route – otherwise you'll always be walking in their shadow.

By forsaking your true identity and becoming somebody else's vision, you are cheating on your dreams. Don't be a shadow-hogging dream-suppressor. Be the trailblazer who lights the way.

Plus, you're a lot more likely to win the race if you're not stuck behind a crowd of wannabes.

Identifying the *Wrong* Path

Do you ever feel like you're trying desperately to be reborn? But you're stuck in an extremely tight vaginal passage and you're the only one flipping pushing?

This is *NOT* the path of least resistance!

I mean there's facing normal challenges, and then there's stubbornly flogging a dead horse, also known as banging your head against a brick wall.

These are not success breeding habits.

I've been this person, trapped in my own dogged determination to do that which does not want to be done. To achieve that which didn't need achieving, and to walk the wrong path – just because I'd set off on it.

And yes, before you start, I get it — it's true that you don't get rich from within the comfort zone. And that overcoming challenges results in growth. We've already done that bit in the previous chapters. *But,* despite these common mantras, it is also a cold hard fact that not every discomfort is a form of expansion. Sometimes, discomfort is just stupidity.

For instance, if a horse touches his nose on the electric fence and gets a jolt – he learns not to do it again. If, however, he repeatedly goes back for shock after shock, what is he? A bloody daft horse, that's what.

He is a glutton for punishment.

Gluttony is excess. So being a glutton for punishment, is excessively punishing yourself.

And so many of us do this, but why?

Well, most of the time it's because we are ashamed to admit that we chose the wrong route, so we stubbornly keep trying to prove we *can* do something—even if we *hate* doing it. Just because we are a daft horse with a sore nose.

The wrong paths may be littered with gold, but if you are feeling all pain and no purpose — you're on the wrong track, my love.

How to Spot the *Right* Path

Your path of least resistance is different. It is, as it says on the tin, the easiest path for you to wander down. It might not be waving a big wodge of moolah at you or entrancing you with a siren call. It could be so discreet that you could completely overlook it at first.

But this path, once you do notice it, is the one that you realise was there all along. It's the 'thing' that arrived with you as a newborn. The only baggage you brought into this world. Your gift.

When you do recognise this place, the entrance to your joyful, soul-growing road. You enter an entirely new portal.

Les Portes

Portal: when you step through a door, and you enter a previously unseen dimension.

So, would you like to follow me into this portal? Beyond the chaos. Back to the beginning of creation. So that you can start afresh. So that every step you take will be in the direction of joy and pleasure.

Imagine that: stepping onto a path that feels as though you have walked alongside it, all of your life?

A few years back, a friend sent me a present in the post. It was a mug, and it had the words 'Joy Bringer' adorned on it. I loved it.

It felt like the best thing that anybody could say to me. I'm not somebody who cares much about my looks – as long as I'm clean and half presentable. Neither am I one who cares for congratulations around achievement. But this really meant something, this compliment — it felt as though

216

I had been turned inside out, and the words were read straight out of my heart.

I realised that was my life's purpose. To bring joy. And to have that noticed by another, well that meant the world to me.

Nevertheless, I spent three years between then, and *that* day in the hospital, bringing *anti-joy* to myself. I was battling defiantly down a path of maximum resistance. I'd been slapped clean in the face multiple times by the great hand of harsh reality, and I had blatantly ignored it. Thinking that if I could believe, I could achieve.

This is, of course, also true: you can achieve anything. But you have to *really* want to — not just to prove that you can.

My heart's desire has always been to write books. To Travel. And to spend time with my family and friends — all of which were being back shelved, because the path that I was on didn't allow for them.

Now, that's not to say that I shouldn't have created Maison Parfaite – of course I should have. It did tick a lot of my fulfilment boxes, and after all, I wouldn't be writing this book about chaos if I hadn't been dealt some property-inflicted whoppers to navigate!

Nevertheless, I could have done it in a way which allowed time for the more important pursuits.

You see, the goal isn't the path. It's to be found at the *end* of the path. And there might be several paths leading to the same goal.

I chose the driven, high-achiever path, which was fraught with comparison, expectation, and overwork. This path had zero room for patience or spiritual and emotional wellbeing. Therefore, it was resistant as hell.

I hopped onto that path when I saw the goal. But I didn't consider the journey — when it's the journey that really matters. Enjoying the ride is everything.

Now I'm not saying that your path will be as silky smooth as a Lindt chocolate bunny – but it won't be a dastardly Were-Rabbit[44] either!

Joyful Acceptance

Just as God almighty will let you know when you're off-piste, you will also receive signs to assure you when you've chosen well.

You'll enter the flow state a lot more easily. Your energy will be higher. You'll tune in to your surroundings and be intuitively guided. Each step will be joyous and self-assured. And you'll start to glow from the inside out.

This is the space for growth, expansion and making an impact. Right here! You can surrender to your higher knowledge, and trust in your way.

You will accept with absolute gratitude and pure grace whatever the universe has in store for you. You're 100% in for the ride.

And, if you find yourself faltering or objecting at any point, just gently remind yourself to relinquish control and to allow all to happen, because, eventually, it is always a blessing.

On the Right Path

I had my awakening in that hospital waiting room.

So I took my blinkers off — and lo and behold, to the side of me was another path. I just had to make a determined leap over to it.

And now, I have resculpted my business, cutting out the bits that didn't serve anymore — some people, some methods, some things.

Along my true path, I've planted the seeds of new growth. I am writing this book! And more importantly I see more of my family.

Joy is now my number one goal. After all, success should be determined by the number of smiles you create – your own included.

Imagine a world where people left for work on a morning with the sole intention of making people laugh and smile, and of bringing joy wherever they went. Now *that* would be a revolution.

For the first time in a long time, I'm excited about business —there's so much good stuff to come, so many parties, events, retreats, and books coming up. All the way along my gloriously rediverted path.

So, my dear, choose *your* path wisely. Remember—the goal *isn't* the path. You might share the same destination as someone else, but your journey should be your own.

Draw your own map. Follow your own signs.

In the words of Fleetwood Mac – *You Can Go Your Own Way!*[45]

You're here for the long run—so make the ride beautiful.

Are you ready to draw that map?

Good. Take my hand, lovely.

Let's begin.

18

The Rebellion Life Philosophy

Stop Conforming. Start Performing.

Chaos has ripped apart the old. And you know the path you *DO NOT* want to be on.

But the new road ahead can seem overwhelming. So, the question is, how do you begin again? What will you do with your blank canvas?

That's where *Rebellion Life* steps in.

What comes next is not only the solution for the sleepless nights. It's the thing that ensures *everything* clicks into place for you.

Rebellion Life is a revolutionary concept for life and business design. Created by me, Sarah McDermott—rebel, free-spirited entrepreneur, party animal, and lover of life!

It's a model that works with the chaos, not against it—utilising pure, heart-centred alchemy to turn the mayhem into a masterpiece.

It's the culmination of the deep work you have undertaken in the *Awakening* module, combined with a set of disciplines and practical workshops, allowing you to etch the most beautiful version of life onto your soul's map.

You see, you can never stop chaos, but you can learn to sit in the eye of your own storm without going dizzy, like a ballerina who teaches herself to pirouette majestically and wobble-free.

From this space, the world is yours.

The birth of Rebellion Life came directly out of my own chaos. Which is just perfect, given that rebellion and chaos go hand in hand. Both are about blasting conformity into smithereens and starting from scratch in a void of pure, limitless potentiality.

Chaos is the wake-up call. Rebellion Life is the conscious choice to take control. Ironically, rebellion puts the order back in.

Imagine waking up *EVERY* morning with that glorious feeling of joyful abundance in your heart.

Priceless.

But also, can you imagine being able to hold that feeling, even when utter chaos swallows you up and spits you out? What would that mean to you?

If you could master yourself to such a degree, then by heck, you'd be a vibrational warrior.

For too long, we have swallowed our deepest desires, in fear of upsetting the expectant crowd around us. We've allowed ourselves to be swept along by a tide of predictable habits—conforming to roles that never quite captured the essence of who we are.

Now you know how to identify and diffuse those patterns, you are on a whole new level of awakening.

Many of us spend years tolerating our careers, just to get money in the bank. Staying in abusive or just plain tedious relationships because it's easier than leaving.

Rebellion Life is about recognising these life drains and daring to make a run for it!

Life is far too precious to be lived on autopilot.

From choosing a career that truly ignites your spirit, to ditching the people, processes and patterns that are holding you back, every choice is a small rebellion against limitation.

This journey is as much about introspection as it is about action. The two must go hand in hand.

Rebellion Life takes everything from the previous chapters, the chaos, the turmoil, the deep emotional digging up, and it offers a framework – a powerful series of practical action steps and exercises – to move you into alignment with your soul.

It's about daring to admit your magnificence.

There's a certain poetry in rebellion. When we choose to defy the mundane and embrace the unknown, we tap into a wellspring of creativity and passion. It is an invitation to look at your own life with fresh eyes and to consider: what does it mean to truly live?

So, whether you are a dreamer quietly defying the humdrum of everyday existence, or an adventurer ready to boldly rewrite your own story, this is an eloquent, heartfelt reminder that the richest life is found not in conformity, but in the beauty of being uniquely, unapologetically yourself.

The richest soul in the world knows that they are the wealth.

The 9 Core Values of Rebellion Life

R - Richness of Life

E - Energy and Flow

B - Boundless Awareness

E - Emotional Mastery

L - Limitless Love

L - Longevity

I - Ikigai

O - Omnipresence

N - Nirvana

Imagine how beautiful life and business can be when they are imprinted with such joy-enhancing values and skills.

R – Richness of Life

Richness is not just your bank balance. Rich is a feeling. It comes from the depth of our experiences.

A truly wealthy life is one where gratitude runs deep, and you wake up every morning knowing that abundance is not something to be chased—it's already in your heart.

I have a friend called Rich—He isn't a millionaire. But he is rich with love. Rich and his wife Trish are welcomed wherever they go. They are loved so much because they are humble, hilarious and never have a bad word to say about anybody. They are abundant in every way that matters— Rich is exactly what it says on his tin. A life such as this is rich as rich can be.

E – Energy and Flow

Life was never meant to feel like an uphill battle. When you align your actions with your truth, you enter a state of flow. It's the path of least resistance. Energy is the undercurrent of everything you do. Are you resisting, or are you flowing?

When energy and flow are mastered, every step feels like a dance, and life becomes a joyful, unfolding masterpiece. So, tell me… Are you a Frequency Ninja?

B – Boundless Awareness

Awareness is the birthplace of transformation.

To cultivate Boundless Awareness is to see life with fresh eyes every day—to question the norms, to challenge your own limitations, and to expand your perspective beyond what you have been taught to believe.

The greatest rebels are awake. They do not settle for a scripted life; they observe, they reflect, they choose. Awareness is the key that unlocks the door to self-mastery.

E – Emotional Mastery

Emotional mastery is not about suppressing what you feel—it is about recognising that emotions are signals, not dictators. When we learn to navigate our emotions with wisdom, we step into true power.

Your peace is non-negotiable. It is the foundation upon which every powerful decision is made. When the world tries to shake you, emotional mastery allows you to stand firm, centred, and unshaken.

L – Limitless Love

At the core of every fulfilled life is love. Not just romantic love, but deep, unconditional love for yourself, your journey, and the world around you.

To rebel is to love yourself enough to demand more – more joy, more authenticity, more meaning. It is to love yourself enough to walk away from what drains you, to pour into what nourishes you, and to surround yourself with people who elevate you.

When you operate from this space, you see the world differently. Love is not a weakness—it is the most rebellious, transformative force there is.

L – Longevity

A truly rebellious life is built for sustainability, depth, and legacy. Longevity means taking care of your physical, mental, and spiritual well-being so you can thrive, not just survive.

It means making decisions that serve both your present and your future self. It means choosing alignment over burnout, vitality over exhaustion, and fulfilment over fleeting success.

A rebel does not self-destruct—they evolve, endure, and inspire. What will your legacy be?

I – Ikigai

The art of living.

Ikigai, the beautiful Japanese word for purposeful living, is the sweet spot where your passions, talents, and contributions to the world align. It is waking up every morning knowing that what you do matters. It is working for the sake of purpose, impact, and joy.

The greatest rebellion is to spend your life doing what you love.

O – Omnipresence

To live omnipresently is to exist fully in all aspects of your life—to be deeply engaged in every moment, to expand beyond limitations, and to leave an impact wherever you go.

To rebel against an ordinary life is to refuse to be confined to a single space, title, or role. It is to embody limitless potential and make your presence felt even in places you have never stepped foot.

A true rebel does not shrink—they expand.

Wherever you go, you are fully there. Wherever you are not, your impact remains.

N – Nirvana

The final destination of Rebellion Life is Nirvana - a state of deep satisfaction and joyousness. This is the reward for stepping off the beaten path, for daring to live authentically, fearlessly, and fully.

Nirvana is not something you chase. It is something you cultivate. It is the moment you realise you are everything you could ever need.

A rebel does not live in longing—they live in contentment.

Heaven is a place on Earth – open your eyes and you'll realise you're in it.

Embracing Rebellion Life

When these nine values become the foundation of your life, everything changes.

- Your time becomes your own.
- Your energy is spent only on what enriches you.
- Your heart is full, your mind is sharp, and your purpose clear.

To rebel is not to resist—it is to rise. To step into the life you were always meant to live.

So, my love, in true rebel style, you've seen the light and offloaded the weights. You are living the Rebellion Life Principles. So let's not put off until tomorrow, that which we can do today—it's time to move forward, and create.

Let's leap straight in with two Rebellion Life exercises that will inspire your next transformation.

Exercise 1: How Rich are You?

This is a beautiful moment now, where you get to sit with yourself and tap into your true genius.

Intuition flows once your 'thinking brain' checks out. And this exercise is brilliant for exhausting your thoughts and opening up the portal to your innermost golden nuggets of inspiration.

It does take a bit of focus though – you need to sit for an hour straight, undisturbed and without taking a break.

From this space you're going to write **100 ways** in which you are already rich.

The first 20 will be easy, the next 40 or so will need thinking about, and the final 40, once your 'thinking brain' runs dry, will be harnessed directly from your intuition – this is the gold. Pure gold. It's a wonderful exercise to do.

Warning: your hand may ache. That's the price of gold, my love!

Exercise 2: Your Rebellion Life Values Assessment

Next up, reflect on each of the Rebellion values, and mark each one with a score out of 10 for your satisfaction in this area of your life right now.

Consider which aspects need working on, and which ones would make the biggest difference to your life if you dedicated more time and energy to them.

These two insightful exercises are going to highlight what really matters to you, what brings you the most joy, and where you feel a sense of lack. And this sets you up perfectly for the next chapter, where you're going to create the antidote to the lack, and see your wildest dreams materialise.

So here it is, love—your compass for life beyond collapse.

The Rebellion Life Philosophy isn't a pretty poster to stick on the wall, it's a way of living, breathing, and making choices that honour who you really are.

So don't just sit there stroking it like a Bond villain's cat.

This isn't for admiring; it's for action.

With these values stitched into your backbone, you'll stop drifting and start directing.

232

Now we move into the space where philosophy becomes plan, rebellion becomes rhythm, and chaos finally begins to play in tune.

19

The Ultimate Fulfilment Vision

'Ooh Heaven is a Place on Earth'[46]

Woohoo!

You have just arrived at one of the most exciting stops on this magical tour of your mind.

This is the place where you get to completely rewrite your story.

It's time for you to create your own Heaven on Earth[46] (with or without Belinda Carlisle).

You've done the deep work around self-awareness. You've been through chaos and exorcised your demons. You've uncovered your unconscious habits, and self-sabotage patterns. You've peeped down the wrong path – and the right path. You now have a set of principles behind you –

exactly the toolkit you need for a reinvention on a seismic scale.

Well done!

That's further than most people will ever go.

Now you get to do the fun stuff!

But, before we dive in, let's think about what that might look like. After all, if you're going to manifest everything you ever wanted, like being wealthy and fulfilled, you need to be really clear about what that is.

So, let's break it down.

What is 'wealth'? And what is 'fulfilment'?

What do these words mean to you?

Wealth

I used to think that being wealthy meant being abundant with money, and I think that most people do. But remember the Rebellion Life Philosophy?

Wealth isn't the green stuff. It's the feeling.

It's the glow – that self-assured contentedness which exudes from every pore of those who've got it. When you look at 'wealthy' people, they have an aura around them that money just can't buy. It's the way their eyes sparkle, the relaxation in their shoulders and the depth of their breath.

Their lightness lifts a room.

But where does that come from? And do you really have to be a millionaire to have it?

In short, *no*.

From a place of poverty, a lack of money is the easiest thing to blame for a lack of happiness. But is that truly the reason?

I don't think it is.

You see, there are seven basic human needs.

Maslow's Hierarchy of Needs[47]

- Physiological Needs – food, water, shelter, sleep, clothing, reproduction.

- Safety Needs – security, safety, stability, health, financial security.

- Love and Belonging – friendship, intimacy, family, community, connection.

- Esteem – respect, recognition, self-esteem, status, achievement.

- Self-Actualisation – fulfilling one's potential, personal growth, purpose.

- Cognitive Needs – knowledge, understanding, meaning.

- Aesthetic Needs – beauty, balance, form, artistic experiences.

It is the satisfaction of these needs, *NOT* a collection of bank notes, stocks, shares or property, that enables the richness of life.

To meet your physiological and safety needs, a certain amount of money is required, but not huge amounts. Once you have financial security, then money just isn't the catalyst for happiness.

What exactly is financial security, anyway? How do we measure that?

Financial security is the state of having stable, sufficient financial resources to meet your basic needs and lifestyle goals—both now and in the future—without constant stress or reliance on external help.

It includes things like:

- Consistent income – enough to cover regular expenses like food, housing, bills, etc.

- Emergency savings – a financial buffer for unexpected costs (repairs, illness, job loss).

- Freedom from debt stress – or at least manageable debt with a clear plan to reduce it.

- Future planning – investments, pensions, or income sources that support long-term stability.

- Choice and control – the ability to make decisions without being restricted purely by money (e.g. choosing work you enjoy, taking time off, going on holiday a few times a year, supporting your family, giving back).

- Peace of mind – feeling safe and confident about your financial position, not just surviving month to month.

There is no mention here of having a Lamborghini or being able to splurge at the casino every Saturday night. Those things are not included. This list does not require you to have a residency on Necker Island to achieve a glow.

If you look back at the list of basic human needs, the majority of the assets in it are acquired via relationship building, connection and self-awareness. Not money. So don't invest all of your focus in the material when you should be aiming for hearts over wallets.

Time is the most precious commodity. It can never be bought back and is therefore priceless. So be really choosy about how you spend yours.

No need to spend years hustling for money, just so
that you can take some time off – when instead you could
simply rework your existing lifestyle for more time off and
still cover your financial needs.

This whole module is about smart orchestration rather than
excess accumulation.

When it comes to 'wealth', be specific, clear and
accurate about what you want. Do you *REALLY* want to be
a multi-millionaire? Or do you want to, first and foremost,
be happy and then let the material riches flow of their own
accord?

Which brings me on to…

Fulfilment

I believe that this is where Branson and crew get their glow.

These guys have been playing full out for most of their
lives to realise a success that is aligned with their purpose.

No matter how crazy their vision might have seemed,
they rode with it. And they won.

This is the reason that they have so much monetary
wealth too – because they found fulfilment—which would
inevitably tap into a flow of all abundance.

So, it was their joy that brought the money. Not the other way round.

I have a friend who climbed Everest recently. She told me about the villagers who live by base camp. They have nothing to their names, but they have a richness of life that is hard to beat. The children joyfully greet passers-by each day—no shoes on their feet, but wearing the smiles of Gods.

They are a connected, loving, friendly community. Just beautiful.

You see, you have the ability to find joy everywhere. As soon as you drop the need to impress others, and you decide to do what you *actually* want to do. When you stop giving hooting toots about what you 'should' be doing, when you align with and start living your purpose,

That is your joy space. Your fulfilment space.

Rebellion Life is a place where folks are definitely not judged on their perceived success.

So, I ask you. What do you really want?

Sit with this thought for a while. And rather than thinking 'I want to earn £200,000 per year' think about why – what would that bring you?

And instead of the money, focus on the end result of having the money – whether that's being able to buy your dream home, or so that you could travel the world, or just because you'd like to feel secure. Whatever the money would bring, focus on how that feels, rather than the actual cash.

Allow yourself the time to daydream – the imagination really is the universal catalogue.

But before you go in for the big order, I'd like you to thoroughly dissect and analyse your intentions – to make sure you are really clear.

You want to meet your ideal partner? Be specific. How would they make you feel? How do they enhance your life? Don't just go for the obvious physical stuff. You don't want to manifest a gorgeous, six-foot twat!

The same with a career, your health, your body. Really start to consider where your priorities lie – and above all, how each of these things would affect your happiness.

We're not going to order an ego massage – this isn't an opportunity to show off to your friends. This is your chance to fully seed your beautiful garden of Eden.

When you're ready, grab a notebook and pen, and let's hop off into another exercise – and this time I'll be doing it with you.

Exercise: The Ultimate Fulfilment Vision

Start by finding a comfortable, warm, quiet space. Perhaps your bedroom, lounge or yoga room – a space where you can lie down, undisturbed.

Leave your limitations and doubts at the door. Open your heart and mind.

Follow this link, www.rebellion-life.com/UFV, to download the guided meditation: we are about to embark on a very beautiful adventure together.

On coming back into the room, stay in your meditative consciousness—you are ready to write intuitively, freely and boundlessly, everything you saw, felt or did in your visualisation. Pour it all into the paper, straight from your heart and soul.

Detail every minute observation that you made in your mind's eye. Remember to include YOU in your vision, ask yourself:

- Who am I?
- What am I here to do?
- What do I switch on each day?
- How do I show up?
- What have I created in my world?
- Who is there with me?

Keep going, don't take any breaks. Write for at least half an hour – the longer, the better.

Write as if it has already happened, as if you are already it. Inject feeling and emotion into it. Really convey the deep physical and mental effects of this transformation with your words. Do not be afraid to declare to the world (or at least to yourself) what you actually want!

"Don't you dare shirk from your own magnificence!"
— The Truth Fairy

Use lines such as:

- 'I spend 6 months of the year travelling to inspiring cities and areas of outstanding natural beauty.'

- 'I am very confident speaking on stages to huge worldwide audiences.'

- 'I have lost 4 stone and am healthier than I have ever been.'

- 'My family and I have moved into our dream home, and we are so incredibly happy.'

- 'I have written a New York Times bestseller.'

- 'I've got 101 puppies!'

They're just examples – although I do quite fancy some of them myself, especially the puppies!

Make yours as wild as you like.

Do not dismiss your dreams. This is your *virtual reality* – the meditation is the head piece. But you are the programmer, and you can populate the landscape at your whim!

Every *thing* in this world began with just a thought, which was then transmuted into substance through focus and right action. Your thoughts are just as powerful as any other creator on our list of great manifestors. Don't forget that.

We're in the land of alchemy. So, pour your heart out, no holds barred, and bring your script with you, my darling, into the next chapter as we connect purpose with financial security.

You've visualised your Heaven on Earth.

Now, let's make it real.

It's time to bring in the wonga—with soul.

Because rich as hell is a vibe. But *rich in alignment*? That's the new rebellion.

20

Purposeful Income

The cure for money constipation

As you float into this chapter, your head full of dreams and a notebook bursting with a life worth living – we're going to pop your feet back on the ground for a moment as we talk about money.

Yes, I know, in the last chapter, I said not to focus on it. That's because I didn't want your intentions to be money-driven. But now that you have created your ultimate vision – it's time to monetise it.

Question: *Do you ever feel that no matter how hard you try, you have a big money blockage that just doesn't want to shift?*

The catalyst for such uncomfortable hold-ups is usually a fatal combo of self-sabotage and a business or career which is completely unaligned with your purpose.

This is where most people declare: *'Oh, but the things I love to do, don't make money.'*

Wrong – that's your belief system piping up again.

As a child from a very working-class background, it was constantly drilled into me that you have to work hard for your money, that work is a chore, and that it causes all manner of stress and physical degeneration.

My own mother and grandmother demonstrated this to perfection—what with their long hours, exhaustion, and work-related ailments—Mum had tennis elbow from repetitive strain as a phlebotomist, and Grandma was riddled with arthritis from being on her feet all day for decades.

It just seemed like work was all about pain and suffering. Whereas my grandad, who rarely worked, could often be found, happy as Larry and pissed as a fart, on his deckchair in the back garden – bottle of whisky by his feet.

He was living his best life. And didn't have to work for the pleasure!

No wonder then, that I went on to create a work-life monster that sent me to hospital and almost drove me to insanity.

It's quite easy for us all to assume that work = woe!

But if you dare to look outside the box, and explore different income genres, you'll see that this couldn't be further from the truth.

Income Genres

There are allegedly, according to the great God Google, only two types of income - active income and passive income.

The Active Income Trap

Active income? What's that? Nobody shouts about this one. Active income means that you are handing over your time in exchange for money, usually in the form of a salary.

It's a means to an end.

The moment you stop physically working, the inflow of cash stops with it. This is the type of income that Mumsy and Grand-mumsy worked for. Or more accurately, slaved for!

And it is still, despite the entrepreneurial opportunities that are available to all these days, the most popular income type.

Most people you know will have an active income.

"Yes darling, active income is basically the hamster wheel—run faster, get more seeds, but you're still in the cage."
– The Truth Fairy

Passive Income

If you are the entrepreneurial type, you'll have heard the term 'passive income' a million times.

It's massively overused to describe various property investment strategies. I can tell you from experience that unless you're placing your money directly in as an investment for a set return, there's nothing passive about it. It's massive passive bollocks.

"Don't call it "passive" if it's draining your soul, darling."
— The Truth Fairy

Now, there are some genuine semi-passive income streams, which become more passive the better you get.

You can learn these by following Lisa Johnson.[48] She is the Queen of Passive Income[48] and at the top of her game, so if you have a talent or skill and you want to monetise it via an evergreen course to make a chunk of money – then learn from Lisa.

One of her clients makes money from hula-hooping![49] Yes, that's right, she loves to hula hoop, and she now has an online business to showcase her skills, which funds her lifestyle. How cool is that?

See Resources at the end of this book for more info on Lisa's courses.

Passive income, when done well, is a beautiful thing.

But get this—not everybody wants to be passive.

For some of us, it's not about the money. We are craving impact over cashflow. We're here to deliver a unique message or to fling ourselves headfirst into something that really matters, and to make a positive difference to the world—we have this deep-rooted passion that just needs to do its thang.

And this kind of pursuit absolutely requires our devotion.

Enter Purposeful Income

I'd like to invite a new rebellious income genre to the table – Purposeful Income.

So, who is this fancy new friend?

Purposeful Income is, quite simply, income generated from passion—it comes about when you put purpose before wealth, and build a business around that.

This business is your baby. Unlike the times when you have followed other people's 'get rich quick schemes', or slaved under employment, this business is a baby that you will love dearly and won't resent spending time with.

It fits in with your lifestyle choices – it doesn't push your human babies (or fur babies) out. It coexists beautifully and holistically. And you want to be with it, to nurture it, to grow it into independence – where it will return the favour and look after you.

Purposeful Income is a beautiful side effect of the good service and joy you produce by bringing to the world that service or product which is in your soul.

This means that Purposeful Income comes with inbuilt good vibes.

You'll love earning this kind of money—money that isn't torturous to earn, the opposite, it's a complete pleasure. And although you might be heavily involved, it doesn't even feel like work.

Why Purposeful Income Changes Everything

You can take that thing that was in your vision – that you saw yourself doing every day – writing, painting, dancing, playing music, being surrounded by puppies! And you can monetise it—it can pay you to have fun doing the things that you love.

There is action involved, yes, absolutely, but this is purpose-driven action, with set intentions. And it feels wonderful.

This is where you go to your quiet space and allow your sparks to start firing. There is always a way to monetise your passion, no matter how obscure, or conversely, no matter how much competition you deem there to be in the industry.

"You are completely unique, and how you deliver your service is completely unique. So, competition is a myth. It's just an excuse."
— The Truth Fairy

Your dream can now become the backbone of your lifestyle. It will feed you—delivering fulfilment and an income, to sustain the growth in your wonderful new garden of expansion.

Pure Monetary Alignment

Hesitation and doubt come from uncertainty. Uncertainty is found on the wrong path. It creates resistance and blockages.

Once you fully align your purpose with your income, you literally insert a spiritual enema right into the source of your wealth blockage - releasing the flow once and for all.

You see, following your passion is always the route to the deepest riches. When you align with your true purpose, and use that to serve others, the universe cannot help but reward you a thousand times over.

And there you have it. You're on the right path. You're living and working through your purpose—channelling your unique gifts to open up a prosperous flow of beautifully aligned income.

It's meant for you.

Love your money, and it will love you back.

Purposeful Income is not only generated from a place of passion, it is also leveraged in a meaningful way, rather than spent frivolously in a flurry of unnecessary mass consumerism.

With Purposeful Income, you appreciate your income and spend it wisely.

Your pounds will be earned and spent with love.

You will cherish your money – earned through great intentions and in good faith. And after all the Rebellion Life work you have done on yourself, you will stop giving it all away, you will know your own worth, and you will allow yourself to hold these beautiful funds, enough to give you a good night's sleep!

Don't get me wrong. You won't hoard from a fear of lack. But you will choose wisely who gets the benefit of your soul-earned wonga.

You see, pounds are like people. Give them a loving environment, and they will procreate.

Show them appreciation - and they'll appreciate right back at you!

Stop working HARD, start working SMART, and respect your wealth.

So before you are tempted to jump on another shiny, entrepreneurial bandwagon, because you feel the need to up-level your net worth and align with whichever wealth guru you are following, please remember that: *your net worth is PRICELESS.*

You cannot put a price on your own head. When people ask what your net worth is, tell them the truth.

Your net worth is the culmination of every lesson you have learned, every process you have mapped, every genius spark that you have had.

It's the gift you carried with you from the spiritual plane into this existence. That rare diamond that nobody else has.

Some event or other could temporarily wipe your monetary wealth. But it cannot remove your ability to recreate it.

When we trim back an unruly tree in the garden, we don't declare it worthless and chuck it on the compost heap. Any gardener worth their salt knows that tree will grow back more abundantly than ever. It'll be the prettiest tree in the garden.

Your net worth is not what is currently hanging on your branches. It's not a Louis Vuitton holdall. It's the intelligence that lies within the seed.

You are priceless, my love. Know that. Don't ever measure yourself with a bank statement.

So, as well as being a priceless diamond (perhaps still in the rough, but not for long), your income shall now be purposeful to boot.

What a joyful existence!

Purposeful Income doesn't flow from a fake version of you. It flows from the most honest, unfiltered, wildly wonderful version of you.

You can't create aligned wealth while wearing someone else's shoes.

Let's look at your own income habits now.

"Awareness is the currency of transformation, babe. Let's audit your income story."
— The Truth Fairy

If you're anything like me, you've probably worn a lot of hats in your life. Jeez, I've been everything from a chip shop assistant to a private investigator!

Some might have looked good on the outside, but felt misaligned on the inside. Yep, my daughters used to tell their teachers at school that their Mumma was a spy! It sounded very cool, but I can tell you, sitting in a car on surveillance for 8 hours on the trot is *far* from glamorous!

So, let's break these down together.

Exercise: Jobs: Money vs. Purpose

Grab your journal and list:

- Every job, role, hustle, or business you've ever done.

- Cross through the ones that sucked the most joy from your soul.

- Star the ones that taught you something you still value.

- Circle the ones that made you feel most like yourself – that's a clue to your purposeful income.

- Now, answer this: What were you craving underneath the money?
  (*Freedom? Safety? Approval? Escape?*)
- What would it have looked like if you'd been paid to be fully yourself instead?

You want to build a life around your truth? You want money that loves you back? Then it's time to stop hiding.

The next chapter shines a light on that diamond. Bringing out all the clarity and brilliance of the radiant jewel that you are.

So, stop apologising. Let's get you on that stage.

Let's bring YOU to the party.

Sunglasses at the ready, it's going to be blinding!

21

Bring Yourself to the Party

I'm a free spirit—I don't conform to the norm.
I'm a spangly-glittered unicorn, in human form.

Do you ever feel like a custard cream in a sea of chocolate Hobnobs?

Custard creams aren't flashy. They're not 'artisan' or triple-chocolate-chip-deluxe. But they're comforting. Classic. Iconic. Everybody secretly loves them—even if the Hobnobs *are* hogging the spotlight.

The world tries to convince you to be a Hobnob. Trendy. Oaty. Instagrammable. Undeniably chic! But actually? There's power in being a custard cream. You're not trying to be anything other than what you are—and that's your magic.

Imposter syndrome can be a terrible thing—a self-built cage of suppression, but just remember that most of those Hobnobs are also feeling insecure in their crumbly, oaty (albeit delicious and chocolatey) skin.

Those fancy pieces are looking at you and envying your retro-uniqueness, your level of experience, and your ability to keep going even when the new biscuits on the block come out!

Be who you are, wear yourself with pride, and give yourself the accolade you deserve for getting to where you are! You're a fricking legend!

Be Unique!

You are the centre of your own world. Whether you admit it or not, you are. And you will never feel fully satisfied, fulfilled, or on fire if you spend your life dancing to the beat of somebody else's drum.

This is your permission slip to stop asking. Come on, when do rebels ever ask for permission? Ditch that etiquette!

Bring yourself to the party. All of you. Even the bits you've been told to quiet down. *ESPECIALLY* those bits.

Too many people shape their businesses, brands, and entire lives around who they think they *should* be, or what will make them seem more acceptable. But the truth is—your power, your magnetism, your freedom—they all live in the place where you stop pretending and start presenting yourself exactly as you are.

The only way to create a business and life that you actually enjoy is to centre it around you. Your values. Your personality. Your weirdness. Your rhythm. Your energy. Your brilliance. Your boundaries. Your unique mix of traits, quirks, and contradictions.

I once employed someone who I later realised was a complete narcissist (yes I know, I have made a few wrong choices!). It came to a head when I asked her to step back from doing something that was absolutely my role—and she exploded.

'This isn't the fucking Sarah Show!', she screamed at me.

In the moment, I thought it was a bit funny, because she was busy making it the 'Her' Show, with endless selfies and cringey posts, all centred around her, on our company social media. But later, I had this realisation: you know what? It actually is the Sarah Show. It's my business. My vision. My story. My life. And I wasn't about to let somebody else's insecurities put me back in the bloody biscuit tin!

It just goes to show that even the most challenging characters have lessons to teach us.

And I want to say that to you, too.

It's *your* life. So, yes—it's the fricking YOU Show. You are the main character, not the sidekick. You're Batman, not Robin.

You're the star of your own movie, not a background extra in someone else's. The crown fits your head, so flipping wear it!

When you try to make yourself small or invisible, to dim your magic and fit someone else's mould, you cheat the world out of something extraordinary.

So for goodness sake my love, wear your sparkle. Be the unicorn in a room full of beige, or the custard cream amongst the choccy dipped fancies. Don't mute your voice. Or swap your tap shoes for slippers just to make others comfortable.

Want to know where to start? Try this soul-mirroring exercise as a beautiful way to do just that.

Exercise

Ask 10 people who know you well—friends, family, colleagues—to tell you:

- How they would describe you to someone else?

- What do they believe your top 3 talents are?

- What do they think makes you special?

You'll be amazed at what comes back. Sometimes we can't see our own magic until someone holds up a mirror. So come on, get yer phone out now and send those messages!

There will be something, at least one talent that you possess, that none of your friends have. Something that makes you, well *YOU*. That one thing that makes your loved ones smile whenever they hear your name. Now that's your thing, honey!

Exercise

Write a 500-word piece about your own uniqueness.

The YOU Monologue – Writing Your Unfiltered Brilliance

- Describe who you are—not just what you do.

- Write about your quirks, values, gifts, and voice. The essence of you.

- If someone were casting you as the main character in a movie, what would the script say?

- Don't worry about grammar or structure—this isn't for anyone else. Write it like you're standing on stage, mic in hand, lights blazing, ready to show the world exactly who you are.

- What parts of yourself have you been hiding, softening, or silencing to make others comfortable?

This piece is your anchor.

Keep it. Read it on the days when you feel small.

It'll remind you of your power, your presence, and your purpose.

Get ready to party and flounce! Show up as you. In all your wonder, in all your realness, without hesitation, own your spotlight.

The truth is—no other bugger can play your part. And the show can't start without you.

REALISE your loveliness, your kindness, your talent, your beauty, your power, your value, your wonderfulness, your uniqueness.

PLEASE appreciate yourself for who you are, because to those around you, you are an absolute treasure!

"If you're gonna sparkle, don't half-arse it. Glitter that shit properly."
– The Truth Fairy

You are the main event. Light up the room. And not just with your tits and teeth!

Now, go work it baby!!!

You've just strutted into your own story. You've glittered like a rebel in a world of beige.

Now what?

Well darling, even Lady Gaga has a schedule, and unicorns need to know where they're galloping.

So, let's get that rebel roadmap down on paper. Not a boring business plan—*a soul-led, freedom-fuelled, you-shaped life-plan.*

The Truth Fairy's got her clipboard. You bring your pen.

22

The Plan

"Those who fail to prepare, prepare to fail."[50]
– Benjamin Franklin

"Those who rebel with a plan? Change the bloody world."
– Sarah McDermott

Now then, my lovely. Every word that you have read, and every exercise that you have completed in this book so far, was in preparation for this section.

Drum roll please… because now is the time where you create your showpiece – the exam at the end of the module. You've worked bloody hard to unravel your mind and make sense of yourself. And to arm yourself with the tools every alchemist requires for masterful manifestation.

This is your opportunity to pull together all of the teachings and quantify them, in one clear, actionable document that will have you swinging from the moon like Dita Von Teese, full of sparkle and joy!

Success in business—and life—is never accidental.

Every visionary movement and every life-changing venture begins with a plan. Yet so many people jump into business with vague ideas and undefined goals, hoping that things will fall into place. They won't.

A great life design plan isn't just a roadmap—it's a manifestation tool. It forces you to think deeply about what you truly want, ensuring that your lifestyle choices and business serve your higher purpose rather than trapping you in an endless cycle of work and resentment.

It provides clarity, aligns your efforts with your dreams, and becomes the blueprint that takes you from where you are now to where you want to be.

The Energy of Intentionality

The act of planning is more than just a strategic exercise— it's creation. When you sit down to map out your business and lifestyle vision, you are setting powerful intentions that begin to shape reality.

Every successful entrepreneur, artist, and thought leader understands that clarity is the first step to manifestation.

And that bloody saying, 'those who fail to prepare, prepare to fail', [50] is so true. I can still hear it ringing in my ears. Like a literary slap round the head.

It was one of the many ventures I've dipped my toe into along this weird and wonderful path. Another non-purpose-driven money-making idea – and like every other shiny penny, I went in gung-ho.

Enter 'Ethical Streetwear-gate'. We knew nothing at all about the fashion industry. Had no connections in garment retail whatsoever. But decided to go in completely blind anyway.

No business plan.

No detailed finance projections.

No investor pack.

No market research.

No nothing other than a naïve dream and a bunch of fluorescent hoodies emblazoned with cheeky one liners like 'Twerkin' 9 to 5' – yes, I know, it's cringe! Middle-aged woman (well, I was in my late 30s) channelling Dolly Parton whilst trying to be 'down with the kids'.

Needless to say, this planless venture flopped.

You see, unlike impulsive nights out – which often turn out to be the best and most hilarious of jaunts – an unplanned business is a sure-fire way to burn money, waste time and make you look a bit of a tit in the process.

And as my cheeks burned red, whilst that solicitor asked about the non-existent plan for this loss-making enterprise, I realised I had committed the heinous act of trying to cook a pie without turning the oven on.

Never again.

You can't just fly at life willy nilly and expect it to catch you. You should know this by now – your manifestation genie will have a right old laugh at your expense if you don't control it. So, control it! With intentions—and a carefully curated plan.

Like a business plan ensures clarity in business, a life plan provides structure for your dream lifestyle, emotional connections, career progression, financial independence, and personal development.

This is your map, your compass, your soul-strategic declaration. It's time to design a life that reflects *your truth*, fuels *your joy*, and honours the *whole of you*.

I know from experience, as demonstrated so succinctly with my streetwear nightmare, that what goes in the plan happens, and what doesn't – well, doesn't!

It's that simple really.

Planning Life and Business

The Rebellion Life Design plan isn't like any other life or business plan, it's completely holistic as it merges both aspects of life and business together into one framework. It's a beautiful translation of your ultimate fulfilment vision.

It takes into consideration every pillar of your life. It prioritises those which are really important – like love, relationships and wellness. And it builds on those which provide security, safety and yes, luxury – because living in that feeling of luxuriousness is our natural state of being. It is your birthright. Don't deny it. Command everything that ever graced your imagination and made you smile.

This is important shizzle. This one document, combined with your Hocus Focus Pocus and Frequency Ninja techniques, will keep you from veering back onto the wrong path.

Whenever you feel yourself falter, pick up your plan, read back through it, reinspire yourself and crack on.

So, let's build it. Not from hustle, but from *wholeness*.

Throughout this chapter, which purposefully has more of an instructional vibe going on—I'll guide you through each section of this glorious new manuscript for your life, but you are going to have to put the work in.

The journalling you have done from the previous exercises will have left you with a stack of priceless material to get this plan going.

When it comes to designing an extraordinary life, this plan is your power tool.

So, without further ado, it's over to you! Pens at the ready again as you formulate your ultimate plan for success, one stage at a time…

Stage 1: Clarifying the Vision

1.1 Rebellion Life Values Check-In

Before crafting your master plan, lets hark back to the exercise in The Rebellion Life Philosophy where you marked each principle out of 10. Remember that one?

Reflect on where you need to shift focus to create more alignment in your life.

The 9 Principles of Rebellion Life

Each of these values should be reflected in the way you build your business and design your lifestyle:

- **Richness of Life** – Structure your life, career and business in a way that allows for rich experiences, as well as financial gain.

- **Energy and Flow** – Avoid forcing things; align with your true flow to create a path that feels natural and exciting.

- **Boundless Awareness** – Stay adaptable and open-minded to new opportunities and insights.

- **Emotional Mastery** – Cultivate resilience and emotional intelligence to lead effectively.

- **Limitless Love** – Choose relationships that feel aligned with your heart and mission.

- **Longevity** – Prioritise balance and sustainability in business and health.

- **Ikigai** – Find the sweet spot where your passions, skills, and business align.

- **Omnipresence** – Create a scalable impact beyond your immediate environment.

- **Nirvana** – Ensure that joy and fulfilment are the primary measures of success.

Integrating These Values Into Your Business & Life Plan

Which values are thriving? Which ones are craving attention?

Use your answers to guide your priorities in every section that follows.

1.2 Define Your Mission Statement – The Heart of your Life and Business

In traditional business terms, a mission statement is a concise declaration of your business's purpose, values, and goals. It should be inspirational, actionable, and future-oriented.

But with the Rebellion Life approach, your mission statement should *also* include:

- **Personal purpose:** What legacy do you want to leave?

- **Lifestyle integration:** How does your business support your dream life?

- **Impact and transformation:** How does your work contribute to others' lives?

This isn't just for business. This is your LIFE'S declaration.

Write. One paragraph that summarises who you are, what matters to you, and how you create impact. And one paragraph on your business's purpose and values. Then merge the two, creating your truly unique *'mic drop, kapow!'* statement. And there you go!

1.3 Craft your Vision

As the creative director of your own life, your vision matters. Take the masterpiece you wrote as your 'Heaven on Earth' and load it with your passion bomb of a mission statement – to birth a stunning written representation of exactly where you are headed. This should flow directly underneath your Mission Statement – so it reads as an expanded version.

Stage 2: Mapping Your Dream Life Domains

You're going to plan your life across six sacred pillars, write each one out to follow on from your overall vision.

1. **Career & Contribution**
2. **Health & Longevity**
3. **Family & Relationships**
4. **Social Life & Community**
5. **Spiritual Fulfilment**
6. **Wealth & Financial Independence**

Career & Contribution

Core Desire:

How do you want to contribute? What energises you?

Purposeful Income Plan:

- How will you monetise your magic?
- What's your dream career or business goal?

- How can you earn in ways that honour your Rebellion
  Life values?

If your job didn't exist, what would you create instead?

Health & Longevity

Body Wisdom:
What routines, rituals, or boundaries keep you well?

Energy Audit:
What drains you? What restores you?

Longevity Plan:

- What does a thriving, sustainable lifestyle look like?

- What are your movement, food, and rest non-
  negotiables?

Optional Add-On: Biohacks, nutrition plan, movement
timetable, grounding rituals.

Family & Relationships

Love in All Forms:

- What kind of partner/friend/parent do you want to
  be?

- What relationships need nourishment or
  boundaries?

Connection Plan:

- What rituals bring you closer to loved ones?
- Where can you release toxic ties?

Social Life & Community

Vibe Check:

- Who are your people?
- Where are your safe, inspiring, liberating spaces?

Friendship Plan:

- What do you want more of—parties, dinners, creative jams, sacred circles?

Visibility Work:

- Where are you hiding?
- Where are you ready to be seen?

Spiritual Fulfilment

Your Belief System:

- What keeps you connected to something bigger?
- What practices deepen your trust in life?

Creative Practice:

- How do you commune with your soul? (Art, music, dance, nature, prayer)

Integration Plan:

- How will you make space for this daily/weekly?

Wealth & Financial Independence

Money Story Audit:

- What patterns are ready to go?

- What beliefs need upgrading?

Income Plan:

- Purposeful Income Stream(s)

- Desired income and impact per month/year

Financial Structure:

- Savings / Emergency fund

- Investments

- Giving / Legacy

"You are not the sum of your bank balance. But baby, you're allowed to have both money and magic."
— The Truth Fairy

Stage 3: Objectives & Strategic Goals

Choose 1–2 bold goals in each life domain.

Use the **SMARTER** model to really niche those goals down:[51]

- Specific
- Measurable
- Aligned
- Realistic
- Time-bound
- Energising
- Reflective of your values

Example: "I will launch my first Purposeful Income offer by [date], serving [ideal audience], earning £[target], in full alignment with my Ikigai."

Stage 4: Time + Energy Planning

Time Management, Time Blocking & Life Balance

A Rebellion Life Plan is not just about financial goals—it's also about how you spend your time. Time is the most valuable resource, and managing it effectively is crucial for success.

- **Time Blocking:** Structuring your day so that the most important tasks get done without distractions.

- **Work vs. Play:** Scheduling intentional rest and creative time to prevent burnout.

- **Energy Management:** Understanding your most productive hours and aligning deep work during those times.

- **Relationships & Health:** Ensuring that your personal relationships and physical well-being are given the same, if not a greater level of priority as business growth.

- **Delegation:** If you hate it, or you're rubbish at it – outsource it. For instance, I'm terrible with tech, so when I want my business plan vajazzling with fancy pics and branding, I hand it over to a Graphic Design Wizardess. I get a super duper fandangled pdf. My wonga helps to keep said Wizardess in all her finery. And my laptop doesn't get thrown out of the window! I get to keep my marbles *and* my time. Bonza!

Weekly Structure:

- Time-block around your priorities (not your to-do list).

- Include space for recovery, flow, play, and mess.

Energy Map:

- Know your rhythms—when do you focus best?

- Schedule soul-work and admin accordingly.

Relationships & Self-Care:

- Block in date nights, playdates, down days, and long baths like your life depends on it. Because it does.

Stage 5: Legacy + Impact

Answer these:

- What impact do you want to have?

- Who do you serve naturally, just by being you?

- What will your grandchildren know you stood for?

Stage 6: Future Projection + Tracking

5-Year Rebellion Forecast:

- Where will you be living?

- What will your business/family look like?

- What are your satisfaction scores on each of the Rebellion Life Principles?

- What's your monthly income?

Include:

- Visual mood board

- Financial spreadsheet

- Key milestones you want to hit year by year

Final Declaration: Your Lifestyle Manifesto

Write a one-page Rebellion Life Manifesto:

- Your values
- Your why
- Your unique sparkle
- Your impact intention
- Your income goal
- Your soul-led legacy

This is your lighthouse. Keep it close. Read it every month. Rewrite it when life shifts.

Through my mentorship programmes, I work with entrepreneurs to craft business plans that turn ideas into reality. My approach ensures each mentee:

- Gains clarity on their vision and structures a business that supports their dream life.
- Develops a rock-solid financial plan that ensures sustainability and profitability.
- Identifies their ideal target audience and unique selling proposition.
- Creates a stunning, investor-ready business plan that makes an impact.

So, there we have it, there's a thoroughly laid-out plan for success.

Woweeee! Your fingers must be aching after all of that writing or typing! Well done my love, for you have just created the backbone of your life.

This plan might take you a while to perfect.

Keep going and as you're on with it, refer back to the previous chapters as many times as you like, and head over to www.rebellion-life.com/lifedesigntemplate and download the FREE template that goes with this section.

Focus on your plan, it might take you a while to finish it. But you're worth it. Don't give up on your dreams. Keep reminding yourself why you're doing this.

There is nothing more satisfying than having the blueprint to your best life at your fingertips.

As each section builds, so will your clarity and your belief in the vision. Each lump of chaotic rubble will float away into the ether as your new foundations are built.

What a magical gift to give yourself – the gift of Foresight, as your pre-committed intentions all come to fruition.

After all my darling, you're not just making a plan; you're making bloody magic!

And if you're super loving this chapter and would appreciate some more guidance, why not join one of our Life Planning workshop events? You know the score by now – head over to www.rebellion-life.com for details!

Right-O! Now all of that practical stuff is done, let's head back in for some more whimsically inspired tales to keep you on the straight and narrow in the Success Module.

Module 5

Success!

Success.

What does it mean to you?

And how would it feel to have all your shit together?

I used to fantasise about success, and have often considered what my measure would be.

When I was younger, back in my private investigation days (yep, that's another story!) I thought I would hit that image of perfection when I could afford to buy all my food at Waitrose, and all my clothes from The White Company.

'Then I've made it', I thought.

But seriously, when you've ridden the rollercoaster of success;

When you've experienced the highs of wealth, and the lows of collapse.

When one minute you could buy the contents of the whole fricking store and the next you could be sat outside with a dog on a string and a tinny in hand.

When you've fought through adversity, when you've shouldered the responsibility of assets and employees,

You realise, after all of this nonsense, that true success can't be bought in a fancy shop.

True success can only be found inside of you.

It arrives, the very moment that your incessant anxiety is replaced by a quiet inner joy.

It's when you find yourself not just calm, but a calmer.

When you are not simply joyful, but a joy bringer.

And when you are more than living, you're an enhancer of life to all of those around you.

To me, success is measured by the number of smiles you create, your own included.

Success is the final module in the CHAOS acronym. It's the natural conclusion of the story.

But it's not the end of the road for you my love—if anything, it's just the beginning.

In this book, it's a module. But in your life, it's a keeper. You've worked hard to get here. Hold onto it.

You're about to learn how to allow, enjoy and maximise your success.

So next time chaos comes your way, even when the storms are swirling all around you, joy is still yours. Always.

Off we go on one more miraculous adventure. Final destination = fulfilment.

I'm going to start by taking you off in a beautiful hot air balloon, removing all limitations. We'll look at the success scupperers that can creep in when you get complacent. As well as clear boundary-setting techniques—ensuring you don't give yourself away, along the way. Then some sound advice on how to keep the knickers on your arse even when the market takes a downturn.

We'll finish with a welcome dose of self-care, proactivity, motivation and next steps, as well as my top feel-good tips to really enhance this experience called life.

You've already found your treasure, my love,

And this is where you get to take it home.

23

Hot Air Balloon

Release the Weights and Rise, Baby!

Just like when Indiana Jones finally gets the treasure (and the girl), after a dalliance or two with death, you now get the prize – success beyond your wildest dreams!

Success doesn't come the moment you finish the plan. It comes the moment you surrender to it. When you stop gripping the ground… and let yourself rise.

The Rise After the Rebuild

You've journeyed through Collapse, found Honesty, Awakened your power, and Orchestrated your plan.

Now… we breathe.

Success in Rebellion Life isn't just about money, milestones, or ticking off goals. It's about becoming light enough to rise.

It's the moment you stop striving and start floating. When alignment outweighs effort. When joy outweighs fear. When you realise that shedding is the strategy.

This phase is about trust. Receiving. Soft power. True fulfilment.

Like all great ascensions, it begins with letting go.

So, before we define success, let's feel it.

A Beautiful Awakening

Some time ago, I was on a power walk with a friend and confidant.

At around the same time, the pair of us had been thoroughly flipped by chaos—and I mean massive, world-changing chaos.

The stuff that forces transformation upon you whether you wanted it or not.

On that particular day, we were making grand plans and discussing the wonderful opportunities that seemed to be flinging themselves at us like we'd never seen before—all born from the chaos.

It's amazing what comes your way once that void has been created.

288

But bear in mind that both of us were still dealing with the aftershock effects of our catastrophic events.

So, there we were, buzzing with ambition, when my dear companion stated the obvious.

'This is crazy, we're talking about this HUGE amount of potential at our fingertips, but in reality, right now, we can't even afford to take our fucking kids on holiday.'

And she was, of course, right.

Both of us had been hit hard financially in the past year—completely sideswiped, and knocked flying into the chaotic void.

We were just about to emerge into a whole new universe—not quite landed yet on solid ground. Both still firefighting and scrabbling to gain our footings.

But my bloody goodness, we were seeing a whole new world of gorgeousness coming into view.

Still, it was more than slightly ironic that we had heads full of multi-million pound ideas, but pockets full of shrapnel.

That contrast—being rich in ideas yet broke in reality—felt absurd.

I looked across at her, and fixed her gaze as we both pondered on the bemusement of it all, when suddenly a magnificent image appeared in my mind. And oh, what a beauty it was!

A majestic hot air balloon, a beautiful, billowing red bubble—with thick ropes, securely attached to a sturdy woven basket, which of course contained my friend and I.

We were firmly on the ground—because of the weights that hung from the sides of our cloud-bound carriage.

And there it was – a lesson straight from the pineal gland. You can be both on the ground AND in the clouds. You can be weighted down AND full of potential at the same time.

This is, after all, a plane of polarity.

If you stand in a weighted basket, of course, it's heavy.

But, if and when you take action and puff that balloon up with air – with hope, with promise, with plans, with success stories yet untold – well, you start to be pulled upwards.

You will feel a resistance as the balloon pulls you up, but the weights hold you down – and it is right here, at this crossroads, where discomfort sets in, and you need to make a choice.

And that's exactly where myself and my comrade were—both at this same juncture – being pulled up and held down by life simultaneously.

It's the most beautiful awakening when you see this. As soon as you recognise yourself in that basket, you know, in stark clarity, that no matter how heavy life feels, you absolutely must keep puffing your blooming balloon up – keep investing time and energy in yourself and focusing on your future.

One day, not long from now, you'll realise that the weights are no longer serving you. And once that balloon is in full force – it will become obvious how to release those pesky lumps of doom.

So, one by one, you take them off. And you rise.

Up, up and away, high into the sky.

There's no fear pulling you back down.

No tribe.

No guilt.

No self-sabotage.

No more past to cling on to.

These weights are now gone.

You are serene, you are free.

Like the truly untethered soul that you are.

High on life, blessed with all that matters and with a position that allows you to look down on life from an entirely different perspective.

Up here, you navigate your own path.

You ride on the air streams. You are warmed by the sun and held up by your beautiful balloon which remains loyal, by your side, forever inflated, enveloping your hopes and dreams.

And that was it. The moment I realised that the remote control to my life was still in my hands. That it didn't matter how dire things might seem on Earth, I am still allowed to dream. To get back up again. To rise from the ashes. Again.

It's not just that you're allowed to dream, you must. Otherwise, you will stay grounded. And wouldn't that be a damn shame, my love!

I cannot express how grateful I am for that gift of awareness. From the moment the hot air balloon popped into my head, the realisation came: we deserve it.

Happiness, that is.

There's no need to hold back anymore.

Shedding is an essential part of renewal and growth.

It's alright doing all this work to puff your lovely balloon up, but you can't move on by holding on to your weights. Now release… and take your rightful position in the clear blue skies of success!

When you do, you'll live as the YOU that you were always meant to be.

The successful, soulful, high-vibing version—floating into view right now.

Over to you now my lovely, what's holding you back?

Exercise: Reflect, Write & Rise

- Which weights can you release?

- What baggage could you lose without missing? What would lighten your load?

- What beliefs, relationships, habits or responsibilities are weighing you down?

- What dreams feel 'too big' that you're ready to reclaim?

- How would it feel to rise without guilt? To succeed without fear?

— The Truth Fairy

Even when you've risen, success has its saboteurs – so in the next chapter, we're going to make sure you don't get stuck in the mud.

Follow me for a masterclass on keeping your head above water!

24

The Pond of OPS

Rising isn't just about letting go of weight. It's about protecting your flow from what's trying to drag you back down—like the bloody Pond of OPS.

There's a place I call 'The Pond of OPS'—and before you ask, *no* OPS is definitely not an abbreviation for opportunities!

Quite the opposite, in fact. This is the place where *anti-opportunity* lives. It's a place where, if you're not careful, *all* of your efforts so far will be completely derailed. The Pond of OPS is an eerie place, haunted with three mega nasties—overwhelm, procrastination, and stagnation—and I've been there more times than I care to admit.

Overwhelm

One of the biggest sappers of success, overwhelm is the state you reach when you look at every plate and worry about how you are going to keep it spinning.

Procrastination

Procrastination is the condition following overwhelm, when you don't know how to start, and the task at hand seems difficult. So, you use delaying tactics rather than taking decisive action.

Stagnation

Stagnation is the end result, if procrastination isn't nipped in the bud.

Let's face it, nobody wants to stagnate.

The word itself conjures up images of decay and rot. Smelly, stagnant water. And like that water, once you lose your flow, you will begin to deplete your energy, your life-force!

Think of your life as a beautiful lake with a flow of fresh water, constantly feeding and nurturing all the growth.

It's an eco-system that contains many mini eco-systems.

You don't need to know exactly how they all work, you don't need to get involved with most of them at all. You just need to ensure that your incoming water flow, and your outgoing outlet, don't get blocked.

Whilst ever the flow continues, you are rewarded with an outpouring of beauty.

But then, one day, you notice something doesn't smell quite right. There is a challenge. Perhaps a tree has fallen and blocked the route. Or somebody has diverted your flow to their lake instead? Or a big fat frog has parked its arse right on your outflow, preventing release.

Whatever it is, this is your lake and there is only you who can deal with it.

The frog has blocked one end, and the tree the other. So which one do you tackle first?

How do you move a great big tree?

And how do you get the rather hostile frog to hop off?

You go into a blind panic, you flap. You can't see the obvious solution—which is always to *just make a start*.

So, you procrastinate. You start MUSTerbating - I must do this, I must do that, but not actually doing any of it!

Then, you make the craziest choice of all – to turn away from your lake and bury your head in the sand so that you don't have to look at it.

If you stay here long enough, your lake will stagnate. It will become toxic. The plethora of tiny eco systems will suffocate and die in the murk. You will be left as the custodian of a large, smelly bog.

Your beautiful lake has turned into the rather grim Pond of OPS. Sound appealing?

Of course not!

Overwhelm can set in when you have a problem, if you don't know where to start. Let's tackle overwhelm before it gets you first.

Let's ensure that you remain an elegant swan on your own lake – composed, calm and graceful, even if your legs are going like buggery below water!

Your Limit

Everybody has a different aptitude for stress. Some of us can handle multiple tasks at one time, and it takes a lot to push us over the edge. Others operate better when handling one thing at once.

There's no right or wrong way. Start by knowing your own limits. And do not allow yourself to get to the edge!

If you can feel yourself getting a bit wobbly, feeling anxious, breathing more rapidly than usual, unable to sleep properly, then rebalancing yourself must be your number one priority.

I speak from experience here. I do have an uncanny ability to multi-task and somehow keep all of my plates spinning, but there have been times when I have fallen face-first into the toxic water because I have shelved my wellbeing in favour of trying to do too much.

Here's a little tale of one such incident.

The Seaside Saga

It was late 2019. We had fallen in love with a beautiful run-down Victorian villa in the unspoilt resort of Robin Hood's Bay.

We purchased her in early 2020, super excited and full of big ideas. We were moving along at pace, ahead of schedule, and then it happened.

The COVID-19 pandemic.

We were, at the time, running six other projects, four for other investors, so there was a lot of expectation there.

Suddenly, we had a reduced workforce, and very limited access to materials. As a result, we had to close the Robin Hood's Bay site for two and a half months as we fought tooth and nail to keep everything else on track through this incredibly challenging time.

This put us way behind schedule.

The first guest pre-booked to arrive was a terminally ill man and his family, this was to be his last family holiday—so there was no way that we could cancel it.

The pressure was on, and my sanity was hanging on by a thread.

We moved ourselves, the kids and the dog, into the building site to help push things on. And the 4:20 am mornings began.

Towards the end of the project, everything just seemed to fall apart. Ten thousand pounds worth of sash windows were dumped in the garden with nobody to fit them. There were renderers who never showed up and plumbers who walked off, leaving jobs half done—every trade seemed to add another layer of chaos.

This was overwhelm on steroids, procrastination knocking at the door, stagnation setting in fast.

But the biggest catastrophe was yet to come: the non-arrival of the lantern roof for the extension.

We needed a temporary roof, so a local window firm sold us some corrugated plastic and said this would suffice.

On the morning of the arrival of the terminally ill man, we were still in full flight, pulling the place together, when suddenly the roof gave way under immense rainfall. With an almighty crash, it caved in, releasing several hundred litres of rainwater.

It flooded the extension, drenching the sofas, the kitchen and even soaked through into the hallway carpet.

It was absolutely devastating.

We needed to act fast. We called the guests, who were due to arrive imminently, and asked if they could delay for two hours, so that we could at least make the space safe for them.

When they arrived, the terminally ill man's wife was in floods of tears.

Her husband needed his machinery to keep him alive. Due to the delay, he couldn't plug in, had a seizure, and had to be resuscitated at the side of the road.

I choked. I couldn't even speak. I just cried.

They stayed amongst the mess, but we gave them a full refund, and another holiday for free.

Still, that didn't repair the intense feelings of loss of control that were boiling up inside me. I was teetering on the brink of a massive breakdown.

Just days after the flood, I finally lost it. I completely went to pieces. I couldn't stop shaking and crying. I couldn't think. It felt like my brain and body were shutting down on me.

I ended up in hospital for 3 days, and then in an Ayurvedic centre for a week, meditating and having treatments to rebalance.

It took about six weeks in all, but I came back to myself.

I survived. And I learnt some very valuable lessons.

We're not invincible, and we're not capable of being repeatedly punched in the gut without dealing with the internal backlash.

This wasn't just a difficult project. It was a living embodiment of overwhelm—and I damn near drowned in that pond—like an ungraceful swan, with her knickers in the air for all to see.

I now take regular time out for mindfulness. After all, success without fulfilment is the biggest failure of all.

If your car battery loses power, you book it in at the garage, right? You wouldn't keep pushing and hope for the best!

So, when you're feeling overwhelmed, book yourself in for a service. Label yourself as 'out of use' for the day, the week, the month, whatever you need.

Turn off your phone. Meditate, do some yoga, get on your Shakti mat, eat a nutritious diet, drink green juices, have a long bath with relaxing essential oils, go for a walk in nature.

By doing this, you'll plug yourself in to the infinite energy source that is available to all of us, and you will re-energise yourself.

And before you say that you don't have time to do this, I'll just tell you that you don't have the time to not do it.

You will be running so much more efficiently afterwards. Your engine will be clean, fast and productive. Why be flat, when you can be fabulous?

Give yourself just one day, and your soul will thank you for weeks afterwards!

"You can't manifest your dream life with a blocked outflow and a dead duck floating in your pond."
— The Truth Fairy

So, how do we drain the pond and get the lake flowing again? Here's my Soul Service Checklist.

Exercise: Sarah's Soul Service Checklist

How to reset when it feels like everything is coming down on you

- Stop doing anything and everything. Take no action at all. Not like rabbit in the headlight syndrome where you're frozen with anxiety. But more like you've given yourself permission to take time out.

- Submerge in cold water if you're having a full-blown anxiety attack.

- Practice diaphragmatic breathing—there are umpteen free tutorials on youtube.

- Be present in the now. Sit and consider what is really going on at this moment – are you safe? Are you warm? Are you fed? Do you have a roof over your head? Take it back to basics and reset your presence.

- Consider the worst-case scenario and dissect it: it's never actually that bad.

- Reset yourself back into a comfort zone with music, memory-jogging TV, gratitude affirmations.

- Avoid stimulants like sugar, alcohol and caffeine – they will all increase your anxiety.

- Go for a walk in nature. Forests and seasides are particularly good. Breathe in and connect with the trees and the ocean.

- Meditate to relieve anxiety until you are back on a higher frequency.

- Chanting meditations are particularly good for re-setting your physiology.

- Be kind to yourself, allow yourself time.

- When you feel ready, ensure you have a maximum of 3 tasks on your to do list at one time. You can't add another until they are done.

- Time blocking: ensure you are prioritising wellness in your diary. DO NOT forgo this in favour of business. It's too important. Remember that without you, there is no business.

- Re-read your Rebellion Life Design Plan – reminding yourself of what you are doing and where your real priorities lie can shrink big scary monsters into little imps.

If you're still struggling to get a grip on overwhelm, go to the Resources section in this book for further help. Or book a FREE call on my website www.rebellion-life.com – don't be alone. We're here for you.

If I'd had this checklist back then, maybe I'd have avoided the fall. Although I suppose I needed the fall to learn the lessons.

Having these tools in my back pocket has saved me more than once in the last few years – and to be honest, the challenges that came *after* this one, have been 10 times more brutal—but I've made it through by coming back time and time again to the lessons gained from this experience.

You see, once you have removed the overwhelm, you can halt the procrastination. And then you clearly see the actions that must be taken.

So, go on my love, use your superpowers to eat that frog and move that huge tree trunk! You've got this. Only you can look after your own lake – but only when you have the power.

If there's one fact I've learned over the past few years, it's this: when you have a health problem, *all* of your other 'problems' suddenly disappear.

Never has there been a truer statement. We totally take our health for granted, until we don't have it anymore – then suddenly we realise that it was the most important thing we ever had.

Don't let it be too late for you when you come to this realisation. God knows it's taken me long enough to 'get it'!

Dying young isn't success – neither is living in chronic pain. (So in the next chapter, we're going to cover this one.)

Let's focus on that one thing that *MUST* be prioritised above all else. After all, it's no good having a glistening lake if you're never going to see it.

Come with me now, darling—there's more clearing to be done, more goodness to weave, more sparkle to sprinkle. It's time to renovate, restore, and rejoice in the most important house you'll ever own: your temple.

25

The Temple

You've released the sludge—now let's make sure the rest of you is still standing—it's no good having 'success' if your body's waving the white flag!

Before we launch into another transformative chapter, I would just like to say that I am not a health guru—I am a yo-yo dieting, peri-menopausal woman, who has danced between peak fitness and too floppy for years.

I mean, moons and moons ago, I did train as a holistic nutritionist—but that was as far as it went.

So I don't profess to know it all on the subject of health.

Nevertheless, I just had to put a chapter in here on health, because what is success if your very being is out of kilter?

I don't care if you have a zillion pounds in the bank – if you're overweight, overstressed and in chronic pain, my love—that ain't success.

Although I am a work in progress myself, I wanted to share the insights that I have gained over the years, in the hope that some of it might help keep you on the straight and narrow.

I have found certain keys to my own health transformation, which I will share with you.

Another thing I have learned along the way is that all bodies are different—and you have to do what works for yours. Some of the guidance below is good for all, but other aspects around specific diets, etc, will need to be tailored to your own disposition.

So read on, absorb it all, but know that, like everything else in life and business, we can share the same goals—but your path to perfect health needs to be yours and yours alone. Try my methods, but get curious, do your own research—and journal your results.

Life is trial and error. And it's only through making the errors and picking them apart, that we find the sweet spot.

The Sacred Vessel

You are the only one with the keys to this sacred vessel. You're the Goddess (or God) of your human shaped soul-home—your temple.

So why do we come here, to this world? For what is just a fleeting lifetime.

I believe that we sacrifice the comfort of that higher place so that we can experience the sensory pleasures and pains, the trials and tribulations that life holds.

Why do we then spend so much time cocking ourselves up?

Well, my dears, that's because many of those sensory pleasures are delicious, fun and addictive. They are also good for masking trials and tribulations.

But most, unfortunately, are not very good for us.

So, here we are. Stuck in an ongoing battle between pleasure and pain. The pleasure masks the pain initially, but then it causes more pain – so we reach again for pleasure. And there the vicious cycle begins.

Of course, we know what is and isn't good for us. But most of our vices are socially acceptable – even celebrated. So it's easy to brush them off.

Safety in numbers, right?

We act like a helpless piggy in the middle, between a holier-than-thou angel on one shoulder and a drunken wild child on the other.

You see, we each hold multiple personalities within ourselves, and our successes in life are *directly linked* to the personality who dominates your decision making at the time.

So who are you listening to? Mary Magdalene or Zelda Fitzgerald?

The trick is to recognise that these alter egos are just that – egos, who in their own ways are trying to keep you safe. The naughty ones by numbing your pain, the nice ones by keeping you away from anything harmful. Both are keeping your limitations in situ.

Once you understand a bit more about these guys, you can silence them and make your own decisions.

So let's kick things off by meeting three of my noisiest egos. You might find you have the same sorts hanging out in your head too.

The Party Animal

Social butterflies, highflyers, dancing queens and rebels – you know who you are. We enjoy the thrill, the exhilaration and the lark of the whole social scene – from throwing wild parties and sophisticated soirèes to sitting outside Café Mambo, sipping cocktails and just inhaling the hedonism.

What an exciting life it is! You feel immortal in your perfect bubble of fun, laughter and debauchery.

Do you know what Sean said to me recently when we were on our way to a do?

'Sarah, you know influencers?'

'Yes, Sean,' I replied with curiosity.

'Well, you could be The Bad Influencer!'

Shock! Horror! I mean, the cheek!

Unfortunately, he was bloody right though.

The Workaholic

Relentlessly striving to prove yourself worthy. Working yourself to the bone. Obsessively focusing on 'the project' to the detriment of all life until it is done.

Recognise this?

It's the downfall of many an entrepreneur—for years you carry on like this, letting real life pass you by.

"Just another hour and then I'll come and watch the film."
– Delusional Workaholic

Reality hits when your kids are flying the nest, and you're still striving.

The Sugar Fiend

Sugar is like smack. This might make you chuckle, but it's actually very true. It is *the* most addictive substance. All I need is one chocolate bar and that's it: I'm off on a rampage, my 'Sugar Fiend' takes over—three weeks later, I've put on a stone.

Sugar, although not listed as a 'hard drug', is as damaging as alcohol and cigarettes. It causes degeneration, organ damage, diabetes, fatty liver disease, and is strongly linked to cancer growth.

When we're under stress, feeling fatigued – or hungover, what do we reach for? Yes, it's sugar – every time! How many times have you walloped a whole packet of Jaffa Cakes into your mouth, without even noticing?

Shortly after my day of reckoning, I was diagnosed with a fatty liver—due to excess sugar in my diet.

Consequently, I'm avoiding sugar like the plague – because, just like the plague, if I don't, it *will kill me*.

The Combo

Together, these three rather intense characters can be exceptionally damaging.

To the outside world it might look like you're achieving great success and having a lovely time celebrating it.

But inside, you're on self-destruct.

You realise you've aged twenty years in just six. You've piled on the weight and completely lost the posture and tone you had in your late 30s.

Buggery bollocks.

It has happened to you.

The inevitable ravages of time. The years of hedonistic abuse. The addiction to overworking. The intense stress and lack of sleep.

They have finally caught up and taken you from a polished vision of youth to a bloated old trollop. (Picture Bet Lynch after a three-day bender[52]—leopard print still hanging on for dear life!)

So, begrudgingly, you put down the box of chocolates (yes, I know it's painful) and the champagne. And you embrace change.

For me, it took a while to sink in. Over the years there have been ups and downs, diets and failures, detoxes and retoxes! All an essential part of the journey to get me here— back on the road to self-improvement.

I've accepted my physical imperfections. But I do want to *feel* good. And quite honestly, I want to live a long and beautiful life.

Whether you've been in the business of self-destruct for 30 years, or just six months, you are here now. So, we can nip it in the bud together.

Let's rebel against degeneration.

It's not just our bodies that we are harming.

It's our minds too. We are switching ourselves off.

Stop Numbing, You Daft Bat

Stop it. Stop shielding yourself from life. It's like going into the cinema blindfolded, and with ear plugs in.

When there's a problem, go cold turkey. *Feel* this real life that is happening.

It's yours.

Own it.

Stop guzzling barrels of wine, and squalloping kilos of chocolate every time discomfort punches you in the guts.

Take the 'peace disruption' for what it is. Because every hardship is a gift in disguise.

Be the rebel who sticks two fingers up in the face of adversity. Not the coward who hides under the table in a storm!

It's time to *stop* with the overfeeding, we are not *foie gras!*

The Seduction of Excess

Why do we think it's cool that we're such excessive guzzle guts?

We use tales of indulgence to endear ourselves to others – we chuckle at the fact that we drank a whole bottle of JD and can't remember a bloody thing.

What we don't say is 'I got trashed at the party because I was worried that nobody would like me' or 'I was so upset when Karen at work called me needy, that I ate my weight in chocolate to comfort my inner child.'

That's not so funny anymore, is it?

To portray yourself as weak.

To admit that the excess was, in fact, a crutch— basically, a metaphorical baby-milk tit for you to suckle.

You might have millions in the bank, but if you're addicted to excess and you've not got your health, what will become of you?

If Henry Tudor is your role model, you've got a problem my love. You're on the fast train to chronic pain.

But, before we look at the solution, there's one little devil we need to discuss briefly.

The Booze Trap

One Year, no Beer. Heard of that? It'll either make you smile with smugness or wince with abhorrence – depending on which side of the coin you sit.

There's been a huge movement towards sobriety in the past few years – and all manner of non-alcoholic tipples have arrived on the market.

I have been hopping on and off that wagon like a frog on acid.

I did spend two years alcohol-free from the age of 38 to 40. And, by heck, it was revolutionary.

You see, alcohol abuse is never good for enhancing joyfulness. It might seem like a good idea at the time (every Saturday night) but then it soon shows its true colours again (every Sunday morning).

You know that feeling when you think you might actually die?

Then, your darling husband insists on divulging the tales of 'last night'—how you were told *THREE* times to get down off the table—and everybody in the pub saw your knickers.

Of course, you can't remember—so you just have to accept that the dazzling display of disgrace is indeed yours.

The guilt.

The shame.

You take a Solpadeine Max and hide under the duvet.

Alcohol is a life-sapping monster. Time speeds up once you pop a bottle—seriously, eight hours pass in a jiffy.

Then you *can't even remember most of it.* And the next day is totally written off.

So, the 2-3 hours that you can *actually* remember costs you 48.

If that's not bad enough, Sean quoted a very sobering phrase to me once. 'Alcohol was invented to keep the working classes down.'[53]

That hit hard. And it made me think.

I am working class, and I don't want to be kept down.

I want to bloody well rise!

You don't see Oprah falling arse over tit out of a taxi with her bum crack on show, do you? You might see her on a yacht, sipping a glass or two of champers—but in a composed, and moderate way.

If it's affecting your ability to rise like Oprah, alcohol needs to be given the boot my love.

It could be just for holidays, maybe? And special occasions, if you insist. But if you're going to get joyful, alcohol ain't for every day – not even every week.

Why not get a buzz from awareness instead?

From being high on life.

You are bubbly and vivacious enough without needing a drink to numb your personality.

That's where I'm at again now. I'm not declaring complete abstinence forever. But alcohol is one of those narcissistic 'friends' who is ok in very small doses, and on rare occasions.

You just shouldn't give her the key to your house.

Alcohol is one piece of your self-destruction puzzle. Combine it with Sugar, Excess and Striving—and you're only heading in one direction.

Maybe, just maybe, it's time to behave?

What can we do to straighten (and dry) you out?

Nutrition

Your body is far more amazing than you give it credit for.

It has the capability to completely replace and renew every single cell in just 7 short years!

This means that if you consume the right quota of nutrients, you can rejuvenate and become biologically younger.

How cool is that? See ya later, Bet Lynch silhouette!

I'm not about to launch into the science here, — that would be a whole new book, but I am going to point you in the direction of Patrick Holford (see references for links to his many insightful books).[54] He is my health guru.

As a teenager, I bought *The Optimum Nutrition Bible*[55] – and he's blown my mind ever since.

What he doesn't know about nutrition, in my opinion, isn't worth knowing. He's a pioneer in his field, a maverick and one of the most engaging teachers I've ever had.

So if you want to recover your health - like I desperately needed to! Follow him.[54] He's our kinda rebel!

Once you know how to look after you, you can't un-know it—and your frazzled body will thank you forever.

Movement & Fresh Air

Your body wants to move.

It can be dancing like a lunatic in your kitchen.

A barefoot walk on the grass.

Or a gentle stretch in the morning.

When we stagnate, our ideas stagnate. Our intuition clogs. Our rebellion dulls.

But when we move? We process. We feel. We release.

Even 20 minutes a day will shift everything.

Walking is sacred. Stretching is sacred. Dancing around your kitchen in your pants is sacred.

When I move my body, my thoughts untangle. My ideas ignite. My sense of being in this skin—this sacred rebel flesh suit—comes alive.

It's time to reclaim your joy. Your circulation. Your radiance.

You don't have to smash out a gym session. But your body wants to move. It wants to flow. Rebel against stagnation—get outside and let the air recalibrate you.

Sleep

The world is a much better place after a good night's sleep.

Sleep isn't just about beauty (although let's be real, sleep is Botox's cousin). It's where your brain gets the chance to reorganise itself, your hormones reset, your stress cycle calms, and your immune system gets a moment to breathe.

Sleep is the temples great repair tool—but most of us don't prioritise it until we crash. Let's change that.

Sleep isn't a luxury—it's your reset button. It's where your subconscious processes everything you've learned so far.

We live in a society that glorifies 4 a.m. starts and 18-hour workdays. Powering through illness.

Working all night with matchsticks in your eyelids? Please.

You're not lazy for going to bed at 9 p.m. You're a bloody legend. Because the truth is: most of us haven't felt properly rested since 1996.

Now? I honour sleep like a ceremony.

Because I've learned that there's no business worth sacrificing my cellular repair for.

Rebel Ritual—Sleep Aids

- Phone off 60 mins before bed

- No TV, news or newspapers for one hour before bed

- Chanting meditation of 'Om'[41] for 20 minutes before sleep

- Ashwagandha or Golden Milk

- An amazing mattress – it'll be the investment of your life!

So off you go, Sleeping Beauty – get ready to take the world by storm!

But before you do, and to ensure you don't cock up your karma before you've even started, here's a mindfulness warrior checklist to ensure your actions *always* result in joy, and not chaos!

Exercise: Your Temple is a Vibe

Before you take any action, ask yourself the following:

- Before I eat this, does it bring well-being?

- Before I drink this, does it bring well-being?

- Before I buy this, does it bring well-being?

- Before I send this, does it bring well-being?

- Before I do this, does it bring wellbeing?

This exercise alone can be life changing—pop it in your phone notes so you never forget!

Health and wellbeing are so important.

This stuff should be prioritised above all else, so to ensure you don't go back to your wicked ways, Madame/Monsieur Mayhem, open up your calendar, and if you haven't already done so, time-block space for wellness—with plenty of time for food preparation, exercise, mindfulness, mediation, and sleep.

Tending to your Temple isn't boring self-care—it's rebellion. It's how you cheat degeneration and dance *longer* in the chaos.

It's boundary number one!

26

Roxy's Rules: Boundaries and Boldness for Rebel Success

She's fierce but loveable, sassy and comical. She gives no woofs but totally gets away with it.

She owns her world.

Enter Roxy, our Bedlington Terrier!

Once you've polished up your Temple, you need to protect it. And no one knows boundaries better than the Great Goddess, Roxy Roo!

Dogs are so good at demonstrating how we should behave.

I mean, if they've done a tinkle on your new silk sheets, perhaps not.

But the humble hound does demonstrate instinctive skills that us humans could do with re-learning.

Roxy is particularly good at this—she's an old girl – the Dot Cotton[56] of the dog world. And although still going strong, she's deaf and as blind as a bat.

So, she's heavily reliant on her super-instincts for acquiring the pleasures in life – namely, food, security, and a fuss!

Roxy is a girl who sure knows what she wants, and she doesn't let anybody get away with ignoring her. She is particularly skilled at setting boundaries, and commanding that things are done in a certain order.

Boundaries are absolutely essential in life and in business.

Having no boundaries means that you have zero control. I'm not for one second suggesting that we bind ourselves with limitations, but we need some—otherwise we leave ourselves open to abuse by others.

I used to be a professional people pleaser—always over giving, both time and money to the wrong 'uns. This would drive Sean insane, and rightly so! He would go as far as hiding a freshly baked cake in the cupboard when said 'friend' was coming round (yes, he did actually do this!)— he was convinced they might squallop every tasty morsel and there'd be none left!

I thought he was a right mean old trout. But really, he was just asserting his defences against the slew of narcissistic, ungrateful, needy ninkynonks that would, one by one, latch on to my trusting nature.

I had soft boundaries. They could see that. And they took full advantage.

I gave them the job.

I lent them the money.

I ran around trying to sort their lives out for them!

Only for them to bugger off—leaving me to deal with whatever chaos they had left in their wake.

I wish I could say this only happened once, but it didn't.

There have been many—including the delightful lot detailed in the previous chapters of this book. It was a pattern.

It has taken me many years, buckets of tears and a huge wodge of cash to develop my 'No twats' boundary.

And Sean is beyond thrilled, now that his wife has a more selective radar and the cakes are out of the danger zone!

However even Sean with his super senses couldn't stop one boundary-less blunder.

This is a sad tale really. But the difference between the human in this story, and the other self-fulfilling chancers, is that this girl was really in great need. And we wanted to help her. Yes—Sean too.

Sean and I were on a night out in Leeds. After leaving a club we wandered down Briggate and spotted a homeless girl by the door of McDonalds. She looked out of place. Dare I say it - she looked fresh, like she wasn't hardened to such a life. So we approached and offered to buy her a meal.

We had a deep conversation. She'd been physically abused by her partner, and she had a young baby - who was now in care. She had nowhere to go.

We had a studio apartment above our detached garage. It was empty.

We arranged to pick her up the next day.

I contacted social services to say we had given her a place to live. We took her shopping and bought her groceries, and a whole new wardrobe. We said that she could start working part time for us.

She was transformed. And the best news? Social services were going to let her have her baby back.

But it wasn't to be.

On Christmas Day we had the whole family around for dinner. My Dad came over from France and brought some fancy champagne. My friend Marie brought all sorts of goodies. The house was jolly and fun. As Christmas should be.

And of course, not wanting our guest to be on her own in the studio, we invited her for dinner.

But it was a temptation too far. That night my friend's purse was emptied, the champagne was stolen, and most of my late grandmother's jewellery was taken from my bedside drawer.

She had disappeared.

The next day she was back in the studio, and she confessed - she said that her partner had come round, that she owed him money (she was a recovering drug addict) and she had been given easy access to the loot in our home.

I felt sick. I was so sad that she had done this, but we obviously couldn't allow her to live in the annex anymore - it was part of our house and shared the same access. We had to choose between giving her another chance, and protecting our own family. Our children were young at the time. She had let her abusive (and it turned out drug dealing) partner into our premises and we couldn't risk that happening again.

I did take her to a women's shelter the next day, with everything that we'd bought her. And we never reported it to the police. But at that point, that's all we could do for her.

I was sad, not just about the stolen items - I was sad for her. That she'd not been able to take the opportunity we had given her. That she wouldn't get her baby back now.

And that was a very harsh lesson on boundaries.

You see, our lack of boundaries allowed the robbery to happen.

And it also gave this lady a temptation that she didn't need. She needed boundaries. All we wanted to do was to help her get her baby back - but lack of boundaries allowed her, in a moment of weakness, to forfeit that opportunity. It was like leaving a small child and a puppy in a room and asking them not to touch each other.

We often think of her, and only hope that whatever she is doing now, she knows somebody once believed in her and believed she was worth saving.

In this instance, Sean and I don't regret trying to help. In fact we are supporters and ambassadors for CEO Sleepout,[57] an amazing fundraising organisation run by our beautiful friend Bianca Robinson.[58] They support regional frontline homeless charities, by having CEOs across the country sleep rough for a night.. See the Resources page if you'd like to get involved.

This is a much better way we can help - raising awareness and funds, whilst leaving the professionals to distribute the means, in a fair and boundary-led manner.

Boundaries are 100% necessary. When we forgo them, not only do we leave ourselves open, we influence negative behaviour in others too. We all know that Children need boundaries—but so do adults. Don't assume others know how to treat you. And don't become the martyr who tolerates life and people.

None of that shite aligns with the Rebellion Life philosophy. So, my love, you need to set your boundaries out for all to see.

Let's get brutally honest, just like Roxy.

What are you tolerating that makes you silently seethe? Who or what is draining your energy like a burst pipe? Where have you said yes when you meant HELL NO?

And more importantly – when did you stop believing you had the right to protect your peace?

It's time to take it back.

You are not here to be a people-pleasing puddle of mush.

You are here to be a bold, beautiful, badass who owns her space like Roxy owns the sofa.

Now here are some firm rules from our best badass bitch, our very own Roxy Roo!

Roxy's Boundary Rules

- If you don't like somebody, tell them to woof off.

- All food belongs to Roxy.

- When you have an itchy arse, wipe it along the carpet unashamedly.

- When forced into the bath, ensure everybody else gets wetter.

- Protect your family fiercely, but bite them if they touch your food.

- If you don't want to walk, just stop until somebody carries you.

- *NEVER* pick up your own poop!

Okay, maybe don't wipe your bum on the carpet—but imagine if we all borrowed just an ounce of audacity from Roxy for a day?

At no point does she hesitate in fear of upsetting the other person or dog. She is solely focused on the end result. Which is entirely based on meeting her needs.

There are four main lessons that I think we should expand on.

1. **Ask Unapologetically** – Roxy requests whatever she wants, loud and proud.

2. **Radiate Self-Confidence** – She gives zero woofs about anyone's opinion.

3. **Master the Art of No** – When Roxy says no, she blooming means it!

4. **Leverage Like a Pro** – She delegates the boring (or smelly) stuff without guilt.

Just think about how these four boundaries could benefit your life now.

Imagine how freeing it would be to be able to say NO to everything you don't actually want to do.

To be able to tell the sleazy guy at work to get the woof out of your space whilst baring your fighting-talk gnashers.

What if you could just ask for whatever you wanted? More money? A hot date? (Without sitting on their knee – only Roxy can get away with that level of brazenness!)

Would that be pretty life changing for you?

Of course it would. Roxy is a Rebel and a half. She's a punky little monkey who appreciates herself, knows her worth, and is totally and utterly connected to her instinctive and intuitive system for surviving and thriving.

She's a badass genius in sheep's clothing – literally!

Exercise: Create Your Roxy Rules

If you want to channel some canine confidence of your own—take out a pen and write down all the ways that bringing these four sacred pooch rules into your life could change your world for the better.

Then go a step further and create your own boundary list. What kind of things would you put on it?

Come on, don't be shy! Write your list of boundaries. Carve your rules in metaphorical stone. And don't just set your boundaries—guard them like a growling terrier in a Gucci collar.

- I will no longer say yes to...

- I will fiercely protect my time by...

- I will only say yes when…

- I will … like Roxy

Think about what is important to you, which rules would you put in place to ensure that you stay joyful?

Take your time on this one—it's such an important stage in re-writing your story and designing your dream life.

Because darling, freedom isn't found in saying yes to everyone else. It's found in saying a fierce, unapologetic no when it matters most.

Boundaries aren't selfish. They're survival. Guard them like Roxy guards her sofa.

Go on, Rebel. Channel your inner Roxy and start barking.

But do NOT pee on my carpet!

And if you thought Roxy was cheeky, you ain't seen nothing yet—keep your knickers on, love, because we're going knee-deep into your smalls next.

27

Keeping the Knickers on Your Arse: Cashflow and Exposure

There are two things we spend – money and time.
You can earn lots of money, and spend all of your time doing it.
Or you can earn time, by spending your money wisely.

Cash is King!

It *must* be. It's on a sign as you enter the Victoria Gate car park in Leeds (yes right before I manifest my spot!).

Every time I see that sign, I wonder what aliens must think of us.

I mean, if an extraterrestrial just happened to pop in, and saw that sign, they might insist on being taken to the great 'King Cash' to discuss our obvious human flaws.

They would probably then sit with K C and give him a few lessons (the aliens in my head are the skinny green accountant types!).

But, despite the fact that I have spent hours pondering this scenario, I never took enough notice of it. Until early 2024, that is – when we got a big sting in the bum, and we almost lost our knickers completely.

I've never really pegged too much importance on cashflow. We always seemed to have a steady stream, and I naively saw the equity we had in properties as a cash fund—believing that it could be tapped into at any time.

How wrong I was!

When unforeseen events affect your credit score, you can't just access cash at the click of a finger anymore.

And that's exactly what happened to us.

After the fraud in 2024, the finance fell through on two ongoing developments—due to the blips on our credit files.

We were left high and dry.

It didn't matter that we were essentially crime victims.

Lenders still closed in and forced us into a worse position—one of them made us fire-sale a property with 40 hours' notice, for £550k less than its market value—even though we'd cleared the arrears on it.

They can be ruthless.

Enter another myth held up high by the property training tribes: *don't leave cash in the bank, always keep it invested in property.*

We learnt the hard way that this simply isn't true.

You need a buffer.

And the bigger your business is, the bigger the buffer you need. Ideally 3-6 months of your outgoing costs should be retained at all times.

If there's one thing for sure, there's always some sneaky little turnip waiting to pull your pants down. Whether that comes in the form of a deviant fraudster, a joyless tyrant of a lender, or God-forbid, a world-wide pandemic.

You can research until your toes curl, but you never know what is around the corner.

So you need to make yourself *corner proof.*

Corner Proofing

There are four pillars for protecting your financial dignity when it comes to the unforeseen.

1. Perspective

2. Multiple Streams of Income

3. Money Loving

4. Financial Planning

1.) Perspective

Perspective is number one. Because once you lose your cool, everything goes to shit.

On the day that fire-sale was completed, I didn't spend the day crying about the fact that we'd just 'lost' £550k.

I thought about how much we'd achieved and where we'd come from — how we'd started with just the house we live in and a couple of buy-to-lets.

I also thought to myself – it will come back. Somehow, that £550k will come back to us (I was starting the manifestation process already).

And actually, as long as we have a roof over our heads, food in our bellies and love in our hearts, then we are rich.

From this calm space I have been able to continue contributing and serving – which inevitably brings returns. You bought this book – there's a fiver back in my pocket already, see!

2.) Multiple Streams of Income

What would you do if you lost your income overnight?

You should *never* rely on just one source.

Once I had cut my teeth in property, I started a mentoring business, which proved invaluable. When the mentoring slowed, the property income flowed, and vice versa.

Now I'm repurposing the chaos to bolster my mentoring business. Rebellion Life is born. And courses, retreats and this book have all come off the back of it.

There's so much you can do to generate more wonga – from pet-boarding (great if you work from home) to online course creation or even selling your excess clobber online.

I once sold a pair of used (but clean, before you ask!) agent provocateur knick knacks on eBay – 'Gangsta' pants they were called. They were too frilly—so off they went.

And get this - the buyer's name was 'Jon-the-Menace'. But I got £55, so I'm not judging!

Think about how you can get a bit of lolly in your locker even when the shit hits the fan.

How can you keep your financial dignity intact?

3.) Money Loving

Money is something that most of us are seriously misaligned with.

We don't connect with it.

We doubt it.

Complain about it.

No wonder it runs a mile!

Energetically, it isn't going to be in your presence if you despise it.

Would you hang out with a friend who calls you dirty? – only if you are Jon the flipping Menace!

Point made.

Go back and re-read Energy, Chapter 16 if you're still hating on the green stuff.

4.) Financial Planning

We are often in a different time zone to our money altogether.

What?

Okay, hear me out, I've not been on the mushroom tea again!

What I mean is that most of us are not present—we are living in the future.

Our minds are consumed by a strange virtual reality, dealing with issues that may or may not arise. Having conversations that may not take place—rather than living in the here and now.

But we spend money in the *present time only,* forgoing future security for a moment of instant gratification. We load up a credit card to acquire new shoes. Giving no hoots about the negative impact on our futures—because we'll be richer by then, right?

Wrong! The seeds you plant now, grow into your future forest. You can't plant an orange and expect an apple tree to grow. Plant the seed of debt, and guess what you'll fruit?

Most of us need a serious chat with our future selves. What would yours say to you?

Put the credit cards down! Unless you're using them as a means to make more money, or you can afford to pay it off every month in full, don't degrade your life.

Basically, if you can't afford it, don't buy it.

Spend your shoe-shopping time building an online course or writing a book to sell your knowledge. Then, buy the flipping shoes with the profit.

One of the few exceptions to this rule is buying property. Most need some kind of lending – but the difference is, this asset will increase in value, and you won't need to sell it on eBay to a deviant sex pest!

Double Bagging

My mother gave me a great tip when I was just a bairn –
always double up when wearing tights—so you don't lose
your gusset.

Ok, any fellas reading this will wonder what the hell
I'm talking about. But ladies, you know all too well how
much hosiery likes to wiggle back down your thighs.

So, protect yourself by wearing an extra pair of super
sturdy pants *OVER* the top of said tights—a hosiery hoist if
you will, so you're not hitching them up every two minutes.
Genius, right?

This is how we need to treat our personal finances too –
with maximum protection.

But it also has to be the *right* protection.

I remember going out for a walk with my doggos, Roxy and
Ralph, one evening. I set off down the lane wearing a short
jumper dress.

However, as I turned onto a particularly busy road, I
suddenly realised I couldn't walk properly.

My knees were restricted.

I glanced down to realise that my body-con tights and
'sturdy pants' were strapped around my knees.

Oh, the shame! As I realised my predicament.

It was rush hour, and there was a queue of commuters all watching my antics from their stationary vehicles—my gathered gusset on display for all to see.

Jeez! I had two giddy Bedlington Terriers, one in each hand, on a very narrow path. I was stuck in an impossible situation.

What was I to do?

I decided the best course of action was to retreat to the woodland lane, taking teeny tiny awkward hops—which took *forever*—until I was out of sight!

I tied the pooches to a tree, yanked the wicked garments back up, and scurried home.

But why did this happen?

How come my mother's trusty method failed me, when it had held me up successfully for years?

Answer: I had chosen the wrong pants.

The selected pair were 'No Visible Panty Line' hipsters – made from a very slick fabric. Coupled with the super sheeny support tights, they had no grip.

They were defenceless against the strong-willed Spanx-esque hosiery warriors advancing down my thighs.

These low-slung knickerbocker un-glories had nothing more to give, and they just slid right down.

So, here's another lesson: Not every support is the right support. It is possible to choose the wrong knick knacks.

Just as not every savings vehicle, or investment vehicle is equal.

So, get it right—your livelihood depends on this.

Do your research.

Only invest in secure investments.

Ensure you're getting the best return on your savings.

Don't just assume that a pant is a pant. Different pants suit different purposes, and a slinky set of smalls isn't going to hold up your world.

Choose well and keep your knickers on your arse at all times!

Here are some very basic rules for maintaining your personal cashflow, follow them and you're in for a smooth(er) ride!

The Rebellion Life Cashflow Rules

Simple truths that protect your knickers AND your sanity.

- Take full responsibility for your own money.

- Never spend more than you earn.

- Love your money – save it and don't give it all away.

- Create multiple streams of income.

- Ask how every financial move will protect your future.

- Optics are the key to financial success – keep your eyes on your finance.

Cash is King, sure, but your knickers? They're the bloody crown.

Because rebellion without cashflow is like tights without pants—you're going down.

And never forget, there's always a manipulative little sausage or a sneaky turnip lurking about, trying to get your knick-knacks down. Guard your crown, they don't deserve it darling.

So, there you go. Whether it's Spanx, silk, or a full granny brief with reinforced gusset—we've kept our dignity and our dosh intact.

Now that your smalls are safe from turnips and sausages, it's time to move into the next chapter, as we lift and separate with your ultimate supporter—the humble bra!

28

Underwires

The support you need to hold your burgeoning life abreast!

A life of fulfilment, joy and happiness, is a full life indeed—and it needs ample support.

Just like a sturdy bra keeps the girls perky, you're going to need scaffolding to keep your *extraordinary* existence up high.

And this level of support is not found in Victoria's Secret, my love.

Non, ma cherie, the scaffold I'm referring to here should be closer to your heart.

Can I just add, for any guys reading this book—your dream has come true darlings—*you are about to get breasts!*

Well metaphorical ones, but still, they'll change your life. Just don't twizzle your nipples off!

There are two major forces behind your ability to peak –
education and community.

Without them, success is theoretical.

With them, it is inevitable.

You see, no matter how often you've survived the chaos,
or how detailed your plan is, you're far more likely to
succeed at doing the do if you have these two powerhouses
at your disposal.

But first, you have to seek them out and declare your
intentions to the world.

Remember what the great JC said – *'ask and it shall be
given'.*[30]

So, don't hang around dithering. Get your biggest
booby-hoister out and fill it with the best stuff.

And darling, I'm going to give you a head start.

The Left Cup—Education

The most obvious way to navigate your path whilst
negating the obstacles—is to *get educated.*

Because education is like a decent push-up bra—it
gives you lift you didn't even know you had, and suddenly
everything looks perkier.

The words within this book didn't just appear in my head one day. A teacher at school taught me to spell. Another one inspired me to write. And countless mentors blessed me with their lessons.

When Sean and I started out in property, we invested an eye watering amount of moolah in training – to make sure we didn't cock it up.

Tony Robbins taught me power mindset[59] —*and how to clap like a manic seal for twelve hours straight!*

I hone my prosperity consciousness by listening to Wayne Dyer[41] and Louise Hay.[9]

My spiritual awareness was ignited by Deepak Chopra.[35] I could go on – my gurus are many.

The truth is that *everything I know* is a mashup of the lessons I've taken from many great masters, combined with my own chaotic lived experience.

In this book I am simply passing on the baton. Maybe in a slightly different tone to Deepak and crew, and with a lot more underwear thrown in for good measure.

But still – I am repurposing those lessons. Dressing them in lingerie, glitter and a smothering of Yorkshire sass, and delivering them to your door.

And that's what we do isn't it?

Learn, win, earn, repeat.

You've already invested umpteen hours in your education—by reading this book.

So why not keep that flow going and ensure your investment is repaid?

Be a winner, not a whinger!

If you choose the right educational platform, mentor, or method—one that aligns perfectly with your true purpose (not another shiny penny). Then you'll be perfectly poised for a fast-track to success.

Leverage the years your mentor has spent perfecting the method and you can reduce decades to days.

That's a lot quicker than learning it the hard way with your knickers round your ankles.

Be successful by following success.

It's a no-brainer, really, and it's the reason why some people will read this book and change the world.

They won't just stop at the book; they'll continue to nourish and expand their minds. They'll arm themselves with the necessary tools, resources, and network to get to the top of their game.

Embrace your education, invest in what matters, and watch how the seeds you plant today blossom into your success tomorrow.

So rebel wisely, learn intelligently, and never stop investing in the version of you that's still waiting to be born.

Investing in your education is like buying lingerie—you don't always want to fork out for it, but when you do, you feel ten times more powerful.

And if you're too tight to invest in learning, don't be surprised when your life looks like a saggy bralette.

The Right Cup—Community

No matter how badass you think you are, humans thrive in a community—even Dolly Parton doesn't go on stage without backup.

Community and contribution are two of the most overlooked but important human needs. Think of how people's faces light up when they feel involved, useful and purposeful.

The deeply joyful satisfaction you get from being part of a tribe is immense—knowing that you are respected and loved, and that they appreciate you for you.

A good community is like a Wonderbra—it gives you lift, shape, and the confidence to strut out without worrying about a wardrobe malfunction.

The right tribe can elevate you up when you're feeling downtrodden. They will remind you, when the chaos hits, just how magnificent you are. And give you the hugs and love you need, to fuel you through to the next level, every time!

They will be your wings.

"Feet, what do I need you for when I have wings to fly?"[60]
— Frida Kahlo

Being surrounded by a crew of cheerleaders, who've been through what you've been through, who've ridden the waves upfront, is invaluable. You'll learn from their hindsight—you'll know when to expect the storms.

And when your back is against the wall, and you feel like you're going to crumble – having a circle to turn to will keep your sanity intact. Sometimes you just need a sounding board – somebody who understands. And, for whatever reason, that's not always your blood family.

When the world is full of ninkynonks intent on causing you harm, you can blast them to smithereens by filling your own heart with love.

In one of my bleakest moments, when an ex 'friend' turned some of my own mentees against me with venomous lies, I was heartbroken. But it was also just then that my real tribe stepped up. Lifted me. Loved me. And made sure I bloody well survived.

But try doing success solo and you'll end up like me—double tights in a woodland—messy, sweaty, and wishing you had backup.

So, I'm not going to leave you hanging here without offering you an opportunity to join one such community. Because even rebels need a gang.

We've been on quite an adventure together, you and I—and I would like to think that this is just the beginning of our road.

I would *love* to see you flourish, to watch as you step into your power and enlighten the world with your unashamed authenticity. So, I'd like to extend my hand once again and invite you to join me in the Rebellion Life community. It's educational, supportive, fun. And it's there to hold you up.

Pop over to <u>www.rebellion-life.com/community</u> and join this joyous community of like-minded, beautiful souls.

Just like popping your favourite Wonderbra on, you're going to feel instantly uplifted and ready to meet the world! No matter how small you might be feeling underneath, you'll be perkier than Dolly on a frosty day.

You're welcome!

Exercise: Strap Yourself In

Alright my love, this isn't homework—it's rebellion. You don't just need knickers on your arse and a structure for your bosoms, you need a plan for the people and places that'll hold you up when chaos tries to drag you down.

Your turn:

- Write down **3 ways you'll invest in your education this year**—courses, books, mentors, even YouTube if it actually teaches you something useful.

- Write down **3 people or communities you can lean on**—and if you can't think of them, don't faff about, get yourself in Rebellion Life.

- Circle one action you'll take **this week** to tighten your straps.

Because underwires aren't comfy, darling—but neither is life when your tits are round your waist.

So, my dear, chaos isn't done with you, it never is—but now you're armed to dance with it.

You've got the plan. You've got the power.

Now go make some bloody magic,

The final chapters await – for one last kick up the bum to see you on your way!

29

Action Pants On!

Woohoo! And off we go. I just love this part of the programme.

For it is time to take all that you have learnt from the pages in this book, every lesson, every golden nugget you absorbed, every intention that you've set in stone—and make it happen!

It's time to don your super-duper fabulous, shiny action pants! Whether you're a wonder-woman or an action man, this is the stage where, unbelievably, most people will give up.

They've enjoyed reading the book. They've chuckled at the anecdotes and maybe even shed a tear as they've been smacked in the face with a dose of reality.

Nevertheless, the tricky bit comes when it's time to take the action.

Some of you will be absolute warriors at this. Others will not – well, not naturally anyway.

That's why it's crucial you keep going back to the toolbox of tricks in Awakening and Orchestration. In fact, you might even need to reverse as far as Honesty if your old self-sabotage trolls pop up for another go.

The techniques I have included within this guide are designed to help you kick your ego into touch when it starts whining that 'it's hard'.

Don't be one of the great ninkynonks who raves about the book, takes zero action, then moans to the world that the model's a load of shite... This is your typical 'the diet doesn't work; it's not my fault' crap. We've heard it a million times. Remember 'It's not my Fault'?

And do you know what, even though I've just said that and outed you in advance – some of you will still do it—*if* you don't follow the mindset and training techniques laid out here.

You get out of life what you put into it, so put your freaking best into it. Don't be another one of the well-intentioned non-starters.

They meditate on becoming a bestselling author but haven't written a word.

They journal about becoming a coach but haven't told anyone they're available.

They draw the vision board and light the candle, but they're still watching bloody TikTok.

This chapter is your gentle but firm command to *get off your arse*.

Remember that fantastic Quaker saying from my tale of manifestation: 'when you pray, move your feet.'[39]

It demonstrates perfectly that no amount of positive thinking alone is going to bring you what you desire in life – until you couple it with action.

"Dreams don't come true on the sofa, love. Pull on your pants and go shake the glitter out of life."
— The Truth Fairy

When I launched my businesses, they didn't happen because the stars aligned. They happened because I set the alarm, made the call, wrote the plan, and went the distance.

I took imperfect action.

I wore the pants.

And not always the glamorous kind, either. Sometimes the action pants are Spanx. Sometimes they're mismatched leggings or work scruffs. . But the point is—*you put them on.*

You do the thing. *You move.*

That's the vibe now. This isn't about hustle. This is about honouring the plan you made when you were clear. This is about showing up for the version of you who finally believed in their future.

Don't betray them now by hovering in hesitation.

Get yourself out there. Be seen. Visibility is viability after all.

Your purpose is not a theory. Your dream isn't a concept. It's a living, breathing thing—and it's time to step into it.

Not next week. Not after one more course or a better time, or a new moon.

Now.

So, make the call. Publish the page. Tell someone what you do.

Start messy. Start scared. Just freaking start.

Because this is what success really looks like: *moving, even when you're not 100% sure you're ready.*

And if there's one lesson that I want to remind you, it's not to put importance on that which is not important.

This is the main cause of suffering and procrastination.

Don't whinge and moan. Drop the self-importance. Don't take yourself or life too seriously. Other than life and love, there isn't much else that is *really* important.

So cut the ties. Shake off the past. Ditch the excuses.

Starting is important—you're allowed to prioritise starting.

Exercise: Get Off Your Arse

Alright darling, time to put your money where your pants are (ok not literally!) But grab a pen and jump straight in:

- Write down one action you've been putting off—and do it within 24 hours. Pants on, no excuse.

- Who can you tell or involve to keep you accountable?

- Make or buy yourself a pair of superhero pants. (*No, I am not joking!*) Take a selfie in them, share it on socials, along with your intended action, or email it to <u>info@ rebellion-life.com</u> so we can add you to our action pants gallery!

- Put those pants on *every time* procrastination blocks your way.

Right-O my love, you ready for your real-life rebellion?

Then let's get those action pants on and dive into the glitterball wonderland that sits there waiting for you to command it.

This is what it was all for—the Collapse, the Honesty, the Awakening, the Orchestration—it's all been leading here: Action = Success!

So come on, Super You!

Let's fly!

I'll see you on the moon.

Cheers to those who walk the walk,
Who balk at those who only talk,
Hallelujah if you're the active one,
Who seized the day, no time to shun
Congrats my dear if you won through,
You persisted, you got there, and you grew
And blessings to all the wondrous souls
Who leapt with faith and hit their goals
You played the game, you took the chance
And now you have the right to dance
The challenges hit, you rode the wave
You accepted it all and held your brave
You didn't go down and blame the world

And that's where your success unfurled

You chose your path, you wrote your story

And now you get to bask in glory

You didn't take note of the cautious tales,

Those laced with fear, of woes and fails

You held yourself high, away from the crowd

And now you're on top, standing proud

Some others may wince as you overachieve

But forgive them, as they have regrets to grieve

Keep shining your light for you light up the dark

Be the peace in the night whilst the crazy dogs bark

Give hope to those yet to embark on their plights

Encourage all to reach their majestic heights

For there really is no better way to inspire

Than showing success built with grit and fire

So, take my heart as I hand it to you

And remember your truth will always shine through

You are brilliance itself, you flow your own groove

So, enjoy it my friend, you have nothing to prove.

Sarah McDermott

30

The Handover

Thank you, my love, from the bottom of my heart.

You don't know how much it has meant to me, to have you in mind as I've written this book. Every memoir, lesson and analogy was created because of you.

Throughout this process I have healed my own trauma, ridden my own chaos, and found my own joy. You've been my therapist as much as I've been yours—and that's a beautiful thing, so *thank you.*

Before I let you go, I just want to share some final words of wisdom to send you on your way with love.

- *Don't take yourself and life too seriously. Park self-importance and righteousness and laugh at life. Put value only on that which truly matters.*

- *Always be completely honest with yourself and others. Sometimes life doesn't go to plan, but it doesn't serve you to deny the obvious.*

- *Regret should be your biggest fear—don't face the horrors of a half-lived life!*

- *Gratitude is the lens that brings life into focus. Let gratitude be your practice, your peace, and your superpower. The more grateful you are, the more attractive you are to everything good.*

- *Aim for JOY. Imagine a world where people left for work on a morning with the sole intention of making people laugh and smile.*

- *Celebrate the success of others, even more so than your own.*

- *Be humble, take responsibility for your own life, and get curious.*

- *Don't be afraid to love unconditionally, laugh out loud, and cry like you mean it..*

- *Be happy with your lot—even if your lot is just a bit.*

- *Happiness radiates, it creates a protective bubble around you that simply doesn't let the shite in. Keep that bubble intact my love.*

Keep these mantras close to your heart, to guide you as you go.

And please remember, there's no need to go it alone - as you've seen throughout this book, the key to success (and failure) is often the people and systems you surround yourself with. This might be the end of our journey

together in this particular book - but really, it's the start
of an opportunity—to embark upon your new path, with
somebody lighting the way.

As much as I've loved writing this, I've also loved the
thought of meeting you, and getting to support you on your
onward journey.

The book has been the journey to the airport - and now
you get to choose whether to board the plane. Destination
Success of course!

So hop on over to www.rebellion-life.com and take a
look at the multiple ways I can continue to support you.
There are CHAOS workshops, courses and retreats -
support, both online and in-person, in the UK and far-flung
destinations! Something to suit everybody.

I'd love to stay with you, and ensure you have the best
chance of success as we bring your dreams into reality.

So now my darling. I'm going to stop writing and hand the
pen over to you. Just like the Oracle hands Bastian his own
fate, in *The Never-Ending Story*.[6]

After all, this is your story – right through this book it
always has been.

I may have written the words, but you have perceived
them in your own unique way. You played out scenario
after scenario in your mind, as we've gone through each

multi-layered chapter. And not another single person—or alien—in this universe has experienced what you have during this process.

You know what to do—take it. Here you go.

Hold it. Start scribing. Write your beautiful life's novel in the truest way possible.

Make it never-ending—and rise.

Go live the life you were born for.

And if you ever forget how magical you are, just look up at the stars and remember:

You. Are. A. Freaking. Miracle.

Lots of love,

Sarah Xxx

P.S—I miss you already - so stay in touch!

References

1. D. Chopra, 'Life is a sexually transmitted incurable condition. The purpose is of human life is to know yourself as the universe.' [post on X], 29 July 2018, available at: https://x.com/DeepakChopra/status/1023569578226536449 [accessed 8 October 2025].

2. *Pinocchio*, directed by B. Sharpsteen and H. Luske, Walt Disney Productions, 1940.

3. *Eat Pray Love*, directed by R. Murphy, Columbia Pictures, 2010.

4. G. Cardone, *The 10X Rule: The Only Difference Between Success and Failure*, Hoboken, NJ, Wiley, 2011.

5. Hesiod, *Theogony*, trans. H. G. Evelyn-White, Cambridge, MA, Harvard University Press, 1914, l. 116.

6. *The NeverEnding Story*, directed by W. Petersen, Neue Constantin Film, 1984.

7. F. S. Shinn, *The Game of Life and How to Play It*, New York, Devorss & Company, 1925.

8. E. Poumpouras, *Becoming Bulletproof: Protect Yourself, Read People, Influence Situations, and Live Fearlessly*, New York, Atria Books, 2020.

9. L. Hay, *You Can Heal Your Life*, Carlsbad, CA, Hay House, 1984.

10. L. Hay, *Mirror Work: 21 Days to Heal Your Life*, Carlsbad, CA, Hay House, 2016.

11. D. Chopra, *The Seven Spiritual Laws of Success: A Practical Guide to the Fulfillment of Your Dreams*, San Rafael, CA, Amber-Allen Publishing / New World Library, 1994, p. 77.

12. *Short Circuit*, directed by J. Badham, performance by A. Sheedy and S. Guttenberg, TriStar Pictures, 1986.

13. *The Reader's Digest*, vol. 51, September 1947, p. 64 — printed as: "Whether you believe you can do a thing or not, you are right." — attributed to H. Ford. Verified in *Quote Investigator*, "Whether You Think You Can or You Think You Can't — You're Right," 2015. Available at: https://quoteinvestigator.com/2015/02/03/you-can/ [Accessed 4 October 2025].

14. R. Pinnick, *SuperGenius – What Is SuperGenius?*, [online] SuperGeniusLife.com, 2014. Available at: https://www.supergeniuslife.com/pages/what-is-supergenius [Accessed 4 October 2025].

15. *Aladdin*, directed by R. Clements and J. Musker, Walt Disney Pictures, 1992.

16. R. Branson, *Losing My Virginity: How I Survived, Had Fun, and Made a Fortune Doing Business My Way*, London, Virgin Books, 1998.

17. N. Hill, *Think and Grow Rich*, Cleveland, OH, The Ralston Society, 1937.

18. D. McKee, *Mr Benn* [Television series], London, BBC, 1971–1972.

19. A. Huxley, *The Doors of Perception*, London, Chatto & Windus, 1954 — title derived from W. Blake, *The Marriage of Heaven and Hell*, c. 1790.

20. J. Dispenza, *Dr Joe Dispenza Official YouTube Channel*, [online] Available at: https://www.youtube.com/@drjoedispenza [Accessed 4 October 2025].

21. The Eagles, *Lyin' Eyes*, on *One of These Nights* [album], Los Angeles, Asylum Records, 1975.

22. D. Kahneman, *Thinking, Fast and Slow*, New York, Farrar, Straus and Giroux, 2011, pp. 80–83.

23. M. Gazzaniga, R. Ivry and G. Mangun, *Cognitive Neuroscience: The Biology of the Mind*, 5th edn, New York, W. W. Norton & Company, 2019, pp. 116–118.

24. *Coronation Street*, created by T. Warren, ITV Granada Television, 1960–present. Character: Vera Duckworth, portrayed by E. Dawn (1974–2008).

25. *Groundhog Day*, directed by H. Ramis, performance by B. Murray and A. MacDowell, Columbia Pictures, 1993.

26. *Willy Wonka & the Chocolate Factory*, directed by M. Stuart, performance by G. Wilder, J. Albertson and P. Ostrum, Wolper Pictures, 1971.

27. *Mary Poppins*, directed by R. Stevenson, performance by J. Andrews, D. Van Dyke and D. Tomlinson, Walt Disney Productions, 1964.

28. *Hocus Pocus*, directed by K. Ortega, performance by B. Midler, S. J. Parker, K. Najimy and O. Katz, Walt Disney Pictures, 1993.

29. R. Byrne, *The Secret*, New York, Atria Books / Beyond Words, 2006.

30. *The Holy Bible*, King James Version, Matthew 7:7, Oxford University Press, Oxford, 1769.

31. E. Nightingale, *The Strangest Secret* [audio recording], Chicago, Nightingale-Conant Corporation, 1956.

32. A. Carnegie, quoted in N. Hill, *The Law of Success*, Meriden, CT, The Ralston University Press, 1928, early chapters.

33. L. Hay, *You Can Heal Your Life*, Carlsbad, CA, Hay House, 1984, p. 63.

34. W. Dyer, *You'll See It When You Believe It: The Way to Your Personal Transformation*, New York, Harper & Row, 1989.

35. D. Chopra, *The Spontaneous Fulfillment of Desire: Harnessing the Infinite Power of Coincidence*, New York, Harmony Books, 2003, p. 17.

36. O. Winfrey, *What I Know For Sure*, New York, Flatiron Books, 2014, p. 15.

37. J. Carrey, interview on *The Oprah Winfrey Show*, aired February 17, 1997, Harpo Productions. Transcript and clip available at: https://www.oprahdaily.com/entertainment/tv-movies/a29498059/jim-carrey-oprah-interview-1997/ [Accessed 4 October 2025].

38. L. Gaga, interview with C. Chocano, *Elle Magazine*, December 2009. Available at: https://www.elle.com/pop-culture/celebrities/a12264/lady-gaga-interview-2009/ [Accessed 4 October 2025].

39. Quaker proverb, often attributed to African Quaker communities and popularised by the American civil rights activist Bayard Rustin. Documented in *Friends Journal*, vol. 47, no. 5, May 2001, p. 22.

40. *The Bodyguard*, directed by Mick Jackson, performance by Kevin Costner and Whitney Houston, Warner Bros. Pictures, 1992.

41. W. Dyer, *Morning and Evening Meditations for Manifesting: AHH & OM Meditations*, YouTube, [online] Available at: https://www.youtube.com/watch?v=3wZTPjpBGe0 [Accessed 5 October 2025].

42. Sefton, 'seft_om (Instagram profile)' [Instagram profile], *Instagram*, n.d., available at: https://www.instagram.com/seft_om [accessed 8 October 2025].

43. B. Dylan, *Blowin' in the Wind, on The Freewheelin' Bob Dylan* [album], New York, Columbia Records, 1963.

44. A. Lord and N. Park, *Wallace & Gromit: The Curse of the Were-Rabbit*, directed by A. Lord and N. Park, performance by P. Sallis, H. Bonham Carter, and R. Fiennes, Aardman Animations/DreamWorks Pictures, 2005.

45. Fleetwood Mac, *Go Your Own Way*, on *Rumours* [album], Burbank, CA, Warner Bros. Records, 1977.

46. Belinda Carlisle, *Heaven Is a Place on Earth*, on *Heaven on Earth* [album], Los Angeles, MCA Records, 1987.

47. A. H. Maslow, *Motivation and Personality* (e-book), New York, Harper & Row, 1987, available at: https://archive.org/details/motivationperson00masl [accessed 5 October 2025], p. 35.

48. L. Johnson, *Lisa Johnson: Business Strategist and Passive Income Expert*, available at: https://lisajohnson.com [accessed 5 October 2025].

49. L. Johnson, *Making Money Online: A Step-by-Step Guide to Creating Passive Income Streams*, London, HarperCollins, 2023, p. 14.

50. B. Franklin, *Poor Richard's Almanack* (e-book), Philadelphia, Benjamin Franklin, 1758, available at: https://

www.gutenberg.org/ebooks/26877 [accessed 5 October 2025].

51. M. Coote, *How to Set Smarter Goals*, London, Pearson, 2016, available at: https://www.pearson.com/uk/articles/2021/01/how-to-set-smarter-goals.html [accessed 5 October 2025].

52. *Coronation Street*, character "Bet Lynch," portrayed by Julie Goodyear, selected episodes 1966–1995; 2002–2003.

53. Commonly attributed to George Orwell, source unverified. Quotation widely circulated online, e.g. *Quote Investigator*, available at: https://quoteinvestigator.com/ [accessed 5 October 2025].

54. P. Holford, *Patrick Holford: Official Website*, available at: https://www.patrickholford.com [accessed 5 October 2025].

P. Holford, *Patrick Holford – Instagram Profile*, available at: https://www.instagram.com/patrickholford/ [accessed 5 October 2025].

P. Holford, *Patrick Holford – Facebook Page*, available at: https://www.facebook.com/PatrickHolford [accessed 5 October 2025].

P. Holford, *Patrick Holford – X (formerly Twitter) Profile*, available at: https://twitter.com/patrickholford [accessed 5 October 2025].

P. Holford, *Patrick Holford – YouTube Channel*, available at: https://www.youtube.com/c/patrickholford [accessed 5 October 2025].

55. P. Holford, *The Optimum Nutrition Bible*, London, Piatkus, 1997.

56. EastEnders, character "Dot Cotton" (later Dot Branning), portrayed by June Brown, selected episodes 1985–1993; 1997–2020.

57. CEO Sleepout, *CEO Sleepout UK – Home*, available at: https://ceosleepout.co.uk [accessed 5 October 2025].

58. B. Robinson, *Bianca Robinson — CEO Sleepout (bio/profile)*, available at: https://ceosleepout.co.uk/about/the-team/ [accessed 5 October 2025].

59. T. Robbins, *Tony Robbins: Official Website*, available at: https://www.tonyrobbins.com [accessed 6 October 2025].

60. F. Kahlo, *The Diary of Frida Kahlo: An Intimate Self-Portrait*, London, Bloomsbury, 1998.

Resources

ACTION PANTS GALLERY

- Email your action-pants selfie to: info@rebellion-life.com.

CALL

- Book a FREE call on Rebellion Life: www.rebellion-life.com.

CEO SLEEPOUT

- Bianca Robinson: https://ceosleepout.co.uk/about/the-team/.

- CEO Sleepout: https://ceosleepout.co.uk.

COMMUNITY

- Rebellion Life Community: www.rebellion-life.com/community.

EVENTS

- Rebellion Life Live Events & Workshops: www.rebellion-life.com.

GUIDED MEDITATION

- The Ultimate Fulfilment Vision: www.rebellion-life.com/UFV.

HEALTH

- Patrick Holford, website: https://www.holfordnutrition.com/.

- My Favourite Books by Patrick Holford:

  - *The Optimum Nutrition Bible: https://www.holfordnutrition.com/product/the-optimum-nutrition-bible-patrick-holford/.*

  - *The Low GL Diet Bible: https://www.holfordnutrition.com/product/the-low-gl-diet-bible-patrick-holford/.*

LIFE PLAN

- Life Plan: www.rebellion-life.com/lifedesigntemplate.

MENTAL HEALTH

- Call the Samaritans (UK & ROI): 116-123

- Helplines & Resources: www.rebellion-life.com/mentalhealth

- AUSTRALIA, Call Lifeline: 13 11 14

- Check this website for suicide hotlines across the globe: https://blog.opencounseling.com/suicide-hotlines/

- USA, Call the Suicide & Crisis Lifeline: 988

- More Resources from the Samaritans: If you're having a difficult time', *samaritans.org*, n.d., available at: https://www.samaritans.org/how-we-can-help/if-youre-having-difficult-time/

PASSIVE INCOME

- Lisa Johnson, Passive Income Queen: https://lisajohnson.com/.

WORKSHOP

- Free Beliefs Workshop Template: www.rebellion-life.com/beliefsexercise.

YOGA

- Sefton: https://www.instagram.com/seft_om